"Patrick Hartin ably reaches into the Pauline letters [...] significant facets of Paul's life in Christ. Readers wi[...] appreciation of a way of living the gospel that has influenced every generation of Christians across the world. The grace and freedom Paul experienced in learning to live in Christ is also explored in a sampling of Christian witnesses who embody the power of the cross and resurrection, the transforming effect of grace, the unmerited gift of faith, and the value of a community of believers bound together in Christ. Perceptive and refreshing."

—Cackie Upchurch, Director
Little Rock Scripture Study

"A Window into the Spirituality of Paul is an excellent and stimulating synthetic presentation of Paul and his spirituality. Fr. Patrick Hartin's perceptive guide to Paul's spirituality treats major aspects of Paul's spiritual vision that are indispensable for Christian life in Christ and his community of faith: the decisive significance of the cross and resurrection; God's transforming grace; faith in Christ; humanity renewed in Christ; a community-oriented spirituality, lived in expectation of the end times. Hartin concludes his valuable study by showing how the four foundational pillars of Pauline spirituality—a new creation through the cross and resurrection of Christ, the transforming power of grace, the gift of faith and the response of good works, and the community of believers as the body of Christ—hold importance in our spirituality today."

—John Navone, SJ
Emeritus Professor of the Pontifical Gregorian University in Rome

"A Window into the Spirituality of Paul is no small peephole into the Apostle. It is, in fact, a large picture window that illuminates the central elements of Paul's spirituality in ways that will be helpful to many people, especially to college students and lay Bible study groups. Consistent with his perspective that the essence of biblical spirituality includes both spiritual vision and everyday response to that vision, he develops a Pauline spirituality that attends to the individual's relationship with Christ while also showing how that relationship can become a pattern for living. An important contribution of the study is the accessible, balanced, and clear way he states and explores Paul's theology—and always with focus on the actual words of Paul. His emphases on the cross and resurrection, the transforming power of grace, faith and good works, the church as the Body of Christ, and humility allow him to write a 'mini-theology' of Paul that provides the basis for contemporary spirituality."

—Rev. Walter F. Taylor, Jr.
Ernest W. and Edith S. Ogram Professor of New Testament Studies
Trinity Lutheran Seminary
Columbus, Ohio

"In his newest book, Patrick Hartin guides us through an often challenging but ultimately rewarding look at the spirituality of Paul. Through a deeper understanding of this early believer's life and experience, we see it as a model for four later-day Christians and for us as well. With such guides as these, and as 'partners with Paul in grace', our spiritual lives can only be enriched."

> —Judy Gritzmacher
> Oratory Center for Spirituality
> Rock Hill, South Carolina

"Those who found valuable insights from Fr. Hartin's *Exploring the Spirituality of the Gospels* will also find great value in this study of Paul. Following a somewhat similar format of this earlier book, Hartin continues to demonstrate how a greater understanding of the contexts within which Paul wrote allows modern readers better insights into how biblical texts might be best utilized by contemporary audiences. These insights would especially apply to those who have questions about Paul's Mediterranean life or are interested in examples of more recent lives that continue to sustain Paul's early examples from the Christian tradition."

> —Ken Stenstrup
> Assistant Professor of Theology
> Saint Mary's University of Minnesota

A Window into
the Spirituality of Paul

Patrick J. Hartin

LITURGICAL PRESS
Collegeville, Minnesota

www.litpress.org

Nihil Obstat: Reverend Robert Harren, J.C.L., *Censor deputatus*
Imprimatur: ✝ Most Reverend Donald J. Kettler, J.C.L., Bishop of Saint Cloud,
Minnesota. July 7, 2015.

Cover design by Ann Blattner. Photo and icon of St. Paul courtesy of Thinkstock by Getty Images.

1   2   3   4   5   6   7   8   9

Library of Congress Cataloging-in-Publication Data

Hartin, P. J. (Patrick J.)
    A window into the spirituality of Paul / Patrick J. Hartin.
        pages cm
    Includes bibliographical references.
    ISBN 978-0-8146-3763-0 — ISBN 978-0-8146-3788-3 (ebook)
    1. Bible. Epistles of Paul—Criticism, interpretation, etc.   2. Spirituality—Biblical teaching.   3. Spirituality—Catholic Church.   I. Title.

BS2650.52.H376   2015
227'.06—dc23   2015003709

Contents

Acknowledgments

This book, *A Window into the Spirituality of Paul*, as its title implies, focuses attention on the spiritual vision that emerges from the letters of St. Paul and his challenge to Christians to respond by their way of life. These two dimensions, spiritual vision and response, are what constitute the essence of biblical spirituality.

Most studies on Paul focus on him as a missionary and the theological message of his letters. Little attention has been devoted to an examination of his spirituality. This book responds to this neglect, most importantly by illustrating the perennial value of his spirituality and especially its relevance and significance for Christians today in the twenty-first century.

A Window into the Spirituality of Paul is written specifically with those in mind who are searching for a deeper understanding of the spiritual message of St. Paul and its relevance for their lives, in particular members of Bible study groups, as well as college students, and those reading the Bible on their own. This present work follows a similar approach to my previous study published by Liturgical Press, *Exploring the Spirituality of the Gospels* (2011). It is my firm hope that this new work will provide a deeper insight into the spiritual vision of Paul's writings and will offer readers direction and guidance for their spiritual lives today.

I wish to express my enormous thanks to Cackie Upchurch, Director of Little Rock Scripture Study, for her guidance and suggestions throughout the writing of this manuscript. As editor, she has been an enormous guide and partner in this work. Not only did she meticulously edit the entire work, but she also provided endless suggestions and comments that have enhanced it. I am indeed indebted to her for the endless hours of painstaking work spent improving this manuscript. I thank her as well for her patience in seeing this project to its completion.

I also wish to thank other editors of Liturgical Press, who over the years have guided my publications, especially Hans Christofferson, Mary Stommes, and Linda Maloney.

Finally, I dedicate this book in gratitude and appreciation to my many students in Bible study groups and college classes. Thank you for inspiring and energizing me with your insights, questions, and enthusiasm for discovering the meaning of God's word for our lives over the course of the past five decades.

Patrick J. Hartin

Spokane, WA

Feast of the Conversion of St Paul, January 25, 2015

Introduction

Context for Exploring Paul's Spirituality

Paul is unique in the pages of the New Testament. Of all the people appearing in the Bible, none is known to us as well as Saul/Paul of Tarsus. Thirteen letters are attributed to him in the New Testament.[1] In more than two-thirds of the Acts of the Apostles (chaps 9–28), Paul is the central figure guiding the establishment and growth of early Christian communities. Practically half the New Testament, then, bears Paul's stamp and influence.

Paul also holds a unique position at the foundation of Christian Spirituality. With the gospels, we have writings from four individual followers of Jesus who have recorded their insights into the life and message of Jesus of Nazareth. In the case of Paul, there is a marked difference. He witnesses the life-transforming experience he had on the road to Damascus that gave his life new purpose and direction. Through the grace of this encounter, Paul illuminates the spiritual meaning of the cross and resurrection for the lives of second-generation Christians. With the gospels, we have a very limited amount of material; with Paul, we have thirteen letters and the Acts of the Apostles to guide our examination. Not only do we have his words, but from the very nature of his correspondence we gain more insight into Paul's character as well as his personal response to the transformative power of Jesus Christ in his life. We can view his spirituality in action.

What Is Christian Spirituality?

While "spirituality" has roots within the framework of Christianity, today the term has branched out to encompass much more. In more recent times, spirituality has grown in popularity within society and has broadened its perspective to such an extent that it is sometimes very difficult to define its meaning. From the influences of psychology and the social sciences, spirituality tends to embrace whatever brings personal well-being and human growth.

In its widest sense, spirituality refers to the life of the spirit as opposed to the material aspect of the human person. As defined in the dictionary, *spiritual* pertains "to the spirit or soul, as distinguished from the physical nature."[2] In its origins the word spirit (*ruah* in Hebrew; *pneuma* in Greek or *spiritus* in Latin) refers to the breath of life or the human spirit that finds its ultimate origin in God. The second creation story in the book of Genesis presents a graphic picture of God as the Master Craftsman who takes soil from the ground and breathes life into his creation and makes of it a living being. "The LORD God formed the man out of the dust of the ground and blew into his nostrils the breath of life, and the man became a living being" (Gen 2:7). In an analogous way in the New Testament, God's Spirit is communicated to the believer who is recreated by the grace and life of God. The writings of Paul draw attention to this twofold understanding of the spirit: the human spirit and God's Spirit. God's grace transforms the human spirit, one's very being. Paul's conclusions to his letters often make this distinction between the human spirit and the divine spirit. Concluding his letter to the Philippians, Paul writes, "The grace of the Lord Jesus Christ be with your spirit" (Phil 4:23).

Biblical scholar Sandra Schneiders gives one of the best descriptions of spirituality: "In short, spirituality refers to the experience of consciously striving to integrate one's life in terms not of isolation and self-absorption but of self-transcendence toward the ultimate value one possesses."[3] This understanding of spirituality conforms to the insights of the social sciences whereby the way in which the human person perceives reality will have a decided effect on the way in which life is experienced and interpreted. From the Christian perspective this means that Christian spirituality is defined above all by the person of Jesus Christ. His person and message animate the experience of Christian life and give it meaning and direction.

Peruvian theologian Gustavo Gutiérrez has provided an interesting insight into the development of a spiritual tradition that is applicable to the spirituality of Paul.[4] He points to three significant moments in the development of a spiritual tradition. In a previous book, *Exploring the Spirituality of the Gospels*, I applied his thought to the gospels.[5] These moments—the experience of encounter, reflection, and prolongation—are equally applicable to Paul's spiritual thought.

Experience of Encounter: In Christianity, every spiritual tradition begins with an encounter with the Lord Jesus. This encounter marks a turning point in a person's life. Paul's life is determined by his encounter with the risen Lord on his journey to Damascus: "[Saul] fell to the ground and heard a voice saying to him, 'Saul, Saul, why are you persecuting me?' He said, 'Who are you, sir?' The reply came, 'I am Jesus, whom you are persecuting'" (Acts 9:4-5). This encounter changed Paul's life dramatically. In his encounter with the risen Lord, Paul is given a mission, "[T]his man is a chosen instrument of mine to carry my name before Gentiles, kings, and Israelites, and I will show him what he will have to suffer for my name" (Acts 9:15-16).

Reflection: After experiencing the Lord Jesus, Paul needed time to reflect on what had happened to him and make sense of this encounter: "I did not immediately consult flesh and blood, nor did I go up to Jerusalem to those who were apostles before me; rather, I went into Arabia and then returned to Damascus" (Gal 1:16-17). Before speaking with others, Paul needed to understand for himself the meaning of this experience. As a student of the famous Rabbi Gamaliel (Acts 22:3), Paul's reflection turned to the word of God, the Torah, and the Prophets to understand how to explain that the crucified and risen Jesus whom he had encountered was now identified as the Messiah of the Scriptures. This turn to personal reflection is part of the process as Gutiérrez says, "To reflect theologically on a spiritual experience means to work through it by relating it to the word of the Lord, to thinking of one's own age, and to other ways of understanding the following of Jesus."[6] Paul's spiritual reflection begins with his own experience that is read in the light of the Scriptures and traditions of the people of Israel. His reflection enabled him to reach new insights in understanding and ways of acting.

Prolongation: Paul's preaching and his letters were the means by which he shared his reflection with others. Through his preaching, as he journeyed from Palestine through Asia Minor to Europe, Paul shared his understanding of the cross and resurrection in light of the Scriptures. His preaching brought many (from the world of Israel as well as from the world of Greece and Rome) to embrace his message and form communities of believers in the Lord Jesus. Through his letters, Paul instructed these communities deeper in his faith in the Lord Jesus and how this should impact their lives. Faith and action go hand in hand. These letters of Paul are invaluable because they speak not only to Paul's first-century audience but they address us as well. In effect, the letters of Paul hand on to us today Paul's spiritual legacy, his spiritual thoughts.

In the twenty-first century, the letters of Paul are more than just past records of his correspondence with the early centers of Christianity he had founded. For Christians, they are *documents of faith.* Throughout his letters Paul hands on his own experience, his reflection, and the transforming power of the presence of God in the Lord Jesus. Paul's intention in his letters is to bring about a *faith response* in the lives of his readers. As with all the New Testament writers, Paul communicates to his readers his own spiritual vision of Jesus and challenges them to respond to this vision in their way of life. "By *vision*, I understand the unifying perspective or picture the biblical writer envisages regarding Jesus and its implications for the life of believers."[7]

These two dimensions of *spiritual vision* and *response* are what constitute the essence of biblical spirituality. Both aspects are clearly evident in the writings and teaching of Paul. In the first instance, Paul lays out the foundation of his faith that rests on his belief in the cross and resurrection of Jesus. He gives a deeper reflection on and understanding of who Jesus is as Lord, Son of God, and Messiah. In the second instance, Paul draws out the implications for believers and the response they are called to give to this belief through their way of life and their actions. The clearest example of the interconnection of these dimensions can be seen in Philippians 2:5-11. Here Paul uses a hymn that is sung in the worship life of the Christian communities that reflects on the person of Jesus Christ. Although he "was in the form of God," he was willing to let go ("emptied himself") of his "equality with God" in order to take on the human form of "a slave" or servant. His humility or emptying went even further to embrace the cross in obedience to the will of his Father. Paul uses this theological reflection on the person of Jesus Christ to instruct believers. As Paul says when he begins this section, "Have among yourselves the same attitude that is also yours in Christ Jesus" (2:5). Paul calls his readers to emulate the humility of Jesus Christ. By taking on the form of slave or servant, Jesus Christ showed that his path through suffering led to exaltation by the Father in the resurrection. The lives of Jesus' followers embrace the same path. Faith in Jesus Christ leads to adopting and imitating the same path of life.

Outline of the Book

Because of Paul's many writings, a richer and deeper insight into his spirituality can be gained than from any other writer in the Bible. This study views Paul's spirituality as a whole while still paying attention to the context of the specific letter when examining particular texts. We wish to gain insight into the foundational key aspects of Paul's understanding of Jesus, his spiritual vision, as well as the spiritual response he calls his readers to embrace in following Christ Jesus.

In structuring this book, I have consciously followed the three-part development of a tradition that Gustavo Gutiérrez identified.[8] In doing so, it is important to note that Paul has not provided a complete spirituality. I am drawing from significant spiritual insights to which Paul gives attention throughout his letters. Further, in the prolongation of Paul's spiritual tradition, Christians over the centuries have embraced aspects of Paul's spiritual vision within the context of their world and time period. In the final section of the book, some Christian witnesses, whose lives demonstrate aspects of Paul's spirituality, will be examined briefly.

In Part One: Paul's Spiritual Encounter of the Risen Lord, attention is given to Paul's Call and Mission (chap 1). The question "Who is Paul?" situates Paul in the context of his world and the spiritual tradition of the people of Israel. At the same time, Paul is uniquely placed as an Israelite who was born outside Palestine in the Diaspora. As such, Paul was steeped in the culture and language of Greece and Rome as well as in the faith of his own people. He stood as it were with feet in two worlds. An examination of Paul's call on the road to Damascus (Acts 9:1-9) shows how much this call transformed his life. From persecutor and archenemy of the followers of Jesus, Paul became the most ardent of Jesus' followers. In this remarkable encounter with the risen Jesus, Paul received a call with a mission to spread Jesus' message to the peoples of the world. I trace Paul's response to his call and mission as reflected in his three missionary journeys. Paul established communities throughout Asia Minor and into Europe, where followers of Jesus could learn about and experience the person of the Lord Jesus. For some fifteen-to-twenty years Paul tirelessly fulfilled his mission to the Gentiles with enthusiasm and joy. His fourth and final journey was as a prisoner to Rome, where his life ended in martyrdom.

In Part Two: Paul's Spiritual Vision: Reflections and Prolongation (chaps 2–7), Gutiérrez's insights continue to shape the exploration into Paul's spiritual tradition. The spiritual experience of encounter leads to reflection and then to a prolongation of the message through Paul's preaching and his letters. I take seriously the definition of biblical spirituality expressed previously as "The search for believers to integrate life through the spiritual vision of those biblical writings that witness to an encounter with God in the person of Jesus and the response required by their transformed life."[9] Attention here is devoted to a thoughtful exploration of how Paul's call both transformed and influenced his spiritual response and way of life and how Jesus' followers are called to respond in a similar manner. Chapter two, The Decisive Significance of the Cross and Resurrection, explores Paul's foundational conviction arising out of his encounter with the risen Jesus. For three years following his spiritual encounter, Paul reflected on his experience in the desert of Arabia and in Damascus (Gal 1:23), drawing out its significance. The essence of his belief centered completely on the crucified Jesus whom Paul experienced as alive and now acknowledged as the Christ, the Messiah, the Anointed One, to whom the Hebrew Scriptures pointed. This insight provided the cornerstone for Paul's spiritual vision and the way of life that he preached. This prompts the question for every reader: "In what sense is Jesus Christ the center and foundation of one's own spirituality?"

Chapter 3, God's Transforming Grace, examines Paul's reflections on his own experience that reveal a deep sense of how God's grace has transformed him from an unworthy recipient into a great apostle: "For I am the least of the apostles, not fit to be called an apostle, because I persecuted the church of God. But by the grace of God I am what I am, and his grace to me has not been ineffective" (1 Cor 15:9-10). This transforming grace gives Paul an insight into the role that suffering plays in his life. A type of identification takes place between himself and the person of Christ. The proclamation of the cross of Christ appears to be a "stumbling block to Jews and a foolishness to Gentiles" (1 Cor 1:23). The consequence for Christians of all ages is to embrace Paul's spiritual vision that sees God's grace as transforming every human weakness in those who are open and respond to God's grace-filled initiative.

Chapter 4, Faith in Christ, explores Paul's understanding of his new life in Christ in terms of the covenantal relationship that God had established. As with the covenant with Abraham, this new covenant embraces all people, not one exclusive nation. Paul contrasts his present spiritual way of life in Christ to that of his former way of life. Previously, Paul had placed great importance on his status as a member of the people of Israel and his faithful adherence to the Torah and its implementation. Now, through his encounter with the risen Lord, this new covenant relationship with God brings him true freedom through Christ's grace.

Chapter 5, Humanity Renewed in Christ, explores Paul's anthropological understanding of the spiritual life. Paul contrasts Christ with Adam in order to highlight the saving grace that came to humanity though Christ. Paul's reflection on Adam shows the state of the world into which Christ came, "Therefore, just as through one person sin entered the world, and through sin, death, and thus death came to all, inasmuch as all sinned" (Rom 5:12). Christ as the New Adam came to liberate humanity from the bondage of sin by inaugurating a new creation (Rom 5:12-21). All who accept him in faith and baptism become a new creature in Christ. Paul describes the inner conflict within the human heart from which Jesus Christ has freed us by his grace (7:14-25). The spiritual consequence for believers is that they are healed through the grace of Christ from this situation of evil in the world and in our human nature.

Chapter 6, Community-Oriented Spirituality, examines the role of the Spirit and the Body of Christ. For Paul, entry into relationship with Christ and rebirth as a new creation take place through the Holy Spirit. The worship that is offered God in Christ is a spiritual worship: "I urge you therefore, brothers, by the mercies of God, to offer your bodies as a living sacrifice, holy and pleasing to God, your spiritual worship" (Rom 12:1). The Church is understood as the Body of Christ (1 Cor 12:12-31). Ethical virtues and demands flow from the understanding that as believers we are all members of the Body of Christ. Significant insights for our spiritual journey are addressed. Paul's great contribution is that the foundation and source of all spirituality for the Christian lies in the life of the Spirit.

In chapter 7, The Goal of the Spiritual Life, attention is given to Paul's eschatological spirituality. With the resurrection of Jesus, the early Christians believed that the end times had already begun. The future resurrection had already broken into our world. Paul's spirituality is understood within this context. The resurrection of Jesus is an indication that what has happened to Jesus will happen to all of us in the age to come. It is a foretaste of what is in store for us who believe. Paul's spirituality gives us the assurance that our journey of life is a journey with Christ and to Christ. The future does not instill fear in us but rather confidence and joy in what lies ahead.

The last part of this book, Paul's Spirituality: Incarnate and Alive Today, draws attention to many significant dimensions of Paul's spirituality. Among these aspects, four foundational pillars or convictions have emerged that hold significance for us today: the cross and the resurrection of Christ (a new creation in Christ); the transforming power of grace; the gift of faith and the response of good works; and the community of believers as the Body of Christ. The final chapter, Paul's Spirituality for Today (chapter 8), reflects briefly upon these four foundational pillars of Paul's spirituality insofar as they hold importance for our spirituality today. In discussing their significance, this chapter illustrates, by way of example from the lives of certain individuals (St. Kateri Tekakwitha; Fr. Stanley Rother; Mother Antonia Brenner; and St. Katharine Drexel), how Christians lived out these pillars of Paul's spirituality.

This exploration through the spiritual vision of Paul and the way it is illustrated in the lives of these heroes of faith has one intention: to show the spiritual importance and relevance for readers today. In every example, God's grace is their foundation. God's grace continues to guide and empower them to lead lives in relation to and in imitation of the cross and resurrection. As with St. Paul, so with the lives of all Christians, the incarnate risen Lord is at the heart of their endeavors. "The grace of our Lord Jesus Christ be with your spirit" (Gal 6:18).

Part One

Paul's Spiritual Encounter of the Risen Lord

Paul's Call and Mission

"Now I want you to know, brothers, that the gospel preached by me is not of human origin. For I did not receive it from a human being, nor was I taught it, but it came through a revelation of Jesus Christ . . . . so that I might proclaim him to the Gentiles."

(Gal 1:11-12, 16)

In the history of Christianity, after the person of Jesus, St. Paul—teacher, missionary, and martyr—is the most influential figure. Every age turns to him for inspiration and guidance. Our exploration of his spirituality begins with the realization that Paul, his letters, and his message emerge from a particular time and historical context. Without such an understanding of Paul's world, it would not be possible to attain an accurate insight into his spirituality. Paul's spiritual message and vision first had meaning for his own time and world. As Christians we believe that the Bible is God's word that speaks to Christians at every age and place, so Paul's spirituality is meaningful for every subsequent generation. Paul is not simply a figure from the past. He is also our spiritual guide and teacher, and his spiritual vision must become incarnate in the twenty-first century.

Who Is Paul?

Spirituality reflects the context out of which it emerged. The same is true of Paul's spirituality. To understand Paul's spirituality it is necessary first to situate Paul in the context of his own world. We begin with a brief overview of the person Paul, his travels, and his place within the framework of early Christianity. Paul, or Saul,[1] as he was known before he became a follower of Jesus, came from the city Tarsus, in south-central Turkey, twenty kilometers inland from the Mediterranean Sea. Tarsus had a rich and interesting history dating back over three thousand years. Very little remains today of the ancient city as the modern-day city, Cumhuriyet Alani, is built over its ruins. At the time of Paul,

Tarsus was an important commercial center. Located at the mouth of the River Tarsus (or Cydnus in antiquity), the city of Tarsus had tremendous commercial importance providing a meeting point for both trade and sea routes that connected the interior of Asia with the Mediterranean Sea. Tarsus was also the administrative capital for the whole region.

Many interesting historical episodes are connected with Tarsus's history. The Roman General Pompey brought the city of Tarsus under the domination of Rome, and in 66 BC the people of Tarsus were granted Roman citizenship. Marcus Tullius Cicero, the famous Roman Senator and philosopher, was Proconsul here in 51 BC. In 41 BC Cleopatra met Marc Antony here for the first time. The "Tarsus Gate of Cleopatra" (or the "Sea Gate") still stands today. According to the legends, Cleopatra sailed up the Cydnus River disguised as Aphrodite and entered this gate on her way to meet Marc Antony. Here Marc Antony and Cleopatra built their fleet that was later destroyed by Octavian (Augustus Caesar) in 31 BC.

In this historically significant and commercially important city, Paul was born (Acts 22:3) around 8 BC, a "Hebrew of Hebrew parentage" (Phil 3:5) and a Roman citizen (Acts 22:25-28). At home in three different cultures (Grecian, Roman, and Palestinian), Paul spoke Greek and Hebrew/Aramaic fluently. With such a background, one can immediately see God's hand behind the choice of Paul as the one to spread Jesus' message beyond Palestine's boundaries.

As a young man, Paul moved to Jerusalem to study his faith more intensely and became a student of Rabbi Gamaliel, a nephew and student of the famous Rabbi Hillel. There is no evidence that Paul was in Jerusalem when Jesus was put to death, but he was there when Stephen was stoned, as the Acts of the Apostles narrates, ". . . they began to stone him. The witnesses laid down their cloaks at the feet of a young man named Saul . . . Now Saul was consenting to his execution" (7:58–8:1). Paul's presence is placed in Jerusalem around AD 34–35.

Through his studies under Gamaliel, Paul became a learned rabbi in his own right. He understood his faith in light of the traditions of the Pharisees ("in observance of the law a Pharisee" [Phil 3:5]). His commitment to his faith led him to view the followers of Jesus with intense hostility. For Paul, they were distorting the traditions and heritage of Israel. He responded by persecuting them (1 Cor 15:9; Gal 1:13; and Phil 3:6). What exactly his persecution entailed, though, is unknown. However, Acts tells us that Paul asked the High Priest in Jerusalem "for letters to the synagogues in Damascus, that, if he should find any men or women who belonged to the Way, he might bring them back to Jerusalem in chains" (9:2). On this journey Paul had an encounter with the risen Lord that gave his life new meaning and direction.[2] He was as committed and enthusiastic for his newfound faith as he had been for his earlier faith. As Paul had journeyed as a Pharisee to Damascus to defend his faith, so now he journeyed throughout the ancient world to spread a knowledge and commitment to the person of Jesus Christ.

Paul, Apostle and Missionary

In relationship to the heritage of Israel, Paul was defined as a Pharisee; in relationship to Jesus' followers, Paul is identified as an apostle and missionary. Paul is a true apostle, as the name itself signifies, "one who is sent" by the risen Jesus, with a mission (Acts 9:15). Paul's apostolic work breaks down into three defined journeys together with a fourth journey to Rome as a prisoner.

First Missionary Journey (Acts 13:1–14:28) [46–49 AD]

After his call, Paul spent three years in the desert of Arabia reflecting on his encounter with the risen Lord. He visited Peter and James briefly in Jerusalem and returned to his home town of Tarsus. From there Barnabas brought Paul to Antioch to help him in his ministry. In the context of a liturgical celebration, the community, under the inspiration of the Spirit, sent Barnabas, Paul, and John Mark (Barnabas's cousin) on a church-sponsored outreach from Antioch to spread the gospel message beyond Syria–Palestine (Acts 13:1-3). Barnabas was in charge of the mission. Acts gives a detailed description of the journey: From the seaport of Seleucia in Syria, they sailed to the island of Cyprus. After crossing the island, they sailed on to Asia Minor (modern-day Turkey), where they visited the cities of Attalia, Perga, Antioch in Pisidia, Iconium, Lystra, and Derbe. In all these cities Paul's message was fiercely rejected by his own people but was well received by the Gentile majority. Retracing their steps, they returned home to Antioch in Syria. In the course of the journey many Gentiles became followers of Jesus. The Church of the Gentiles emerged.

Council of Jerusalem (Acts 15) [49 AD]

The incorporation of believers from the Gentile world sparked a heated discussion within the church in Jerusalem. "What was required for believers from the Gentile world to become members of the church?" The Jerusalem church demanded that they should abide by all the obligations, laws, and way of life of the people of Israel. In contrast, Paul's view was that Jesus' death and resurrection had freed his followers from the stipulations of the Mosaic Law. After much discussion (Acts 15), the apostles decided that the prescriptions of the Law of Moses should not be imposed upon the Gentiles, including the ritual of circumcision for males (Acts 15:6-29). Through baptism they became Christians and belonged to Christ. One's whole life was meant to be led in relationship to Christ. The apostles wrote a letter explaining to the churches their unanimous agreement. Paul and Barnabas returned to Antioch with the letter. This decision was momentous for the future direction of the Christian church.

Second Missionary Journey (Acts 15:36–18:22) [49–52 AD]

After a dispute concerning John Mark, Paul and Barnabas separated. Choosing Silas as his traveling companion, Paul went overland to visit those Christian communities he had founded in Asia Minor: Iconium, Derbe, and Lystra. While in Lystra, Paul was joined by a young man, Timothy (the son of a Jewish mother and a pagan father), who would become an influential person in the early church. Paul had Timothy circumcised so that they could continue their mission of preaching, first to the Jews in their synagogues and then to the Gentiles. They traveled across central Asia Minor and reached the coastal town of Troas, where Paul had a dream of a Macedonian begging him, "Come over to Macedonia and help us" (Acts 16:9). Paul interpreted this dream to mean that God was calling them to cross over and preach the Good News on the continent of Europe for the first time. Philippi, the first church established there, was to become a very vibrant community. From Philippi, Paul journeyed through Greece establishing a number of Christian communities, such as Thessalonica. On reaching Athens, the cultural capital of the Mediterranean world, Paul engaged in discussion with some leading Greek philosophers. However, when Paul preached of the cross and resurrection, the Athenians were unable to accept his central message and walked away. Finally, Paul reached Corinth, where he stayed for a year and a half. In Corinth, Paul was brought before the Roman proconsul of the Senatorial Province of Achaia, Gallio, on charges that he was promoting an unlawful religion. This event is noteworthy as it provides a reliable chronological detail. An inscription has been found in Delphi that mentions this Gallio and identifies him as proconsul in Corinth during the years 51 and 53. This evidence dates Paul's stay in Corinth to these years (51–52). Hearing about concerns back in Thessalonica, Paul writes a letter explaining aspects of the Christian faith that were causing confusion. So began Paul's epistolary career. From Corinth, Paul sailed home to Palestine. He landed in the port city of Caesarea Maritima and went up to visit the church of Jerusalem before returning to his home church of Antioch.

Third Missionary Journey (Acts 18:23–21:16) [53 58 AD]

Paul started out again from Antioch intent on visiting the city of Ephesus, capital of the Roman Province of Asia. During his three-year stay there (Acts 20:31), Paul wrote a number of letters (such as the two letters to the Corinthians, Philemon, and Philippians). The famous temple of Artemis, the Artemision, one of the seven wonders of the ancient world, stood proudly in the city of Ephesus. Worshipers came here from all over Greece and the ancient world. Paul's preaching against the worship of idols caused a great disturbance in Ephesus and forced him to leave. He journeyed throughout Greece revisiting those churches he had established on his second journey. He stayed in Corinth again for three months, during which time he wrote the letters to the Romans and Galatians. On his return journey to Palestine, Paul arrived at the port city of Miletus and called the elders from Ephesus to join him there. In his farewell speech, Paul intimated that he would not see them again (20:25). He sailed home to Palestine, disembarked at the port of Caesarea Maritima and traveled up to Jerusalem, where he visited the temple. His presence caused a riot as he was accused of bringing some pagans into the temple area. The Romans intervened and arrested Paul. Paul remained in prison for two years.

After invoking his privilege as a Roman citizen, he appealed to the Roman Emperor Nero to hear his case. He was sent to Rome with a centurion to accompany him. After a difficult sea journey involving being shipwrecked off the island of Malta (27:1–28:16), Paul arrived in Rome, where he stayed under house arrest for two years awaiting trial (28:30). At this point Luke ends his narrative of the Acts of the Apostles. Nothing is said about the outcome of his trial (28:30-31). There are legends that narrate that Paul was released and journeyed farther to Spain. Historical evidence clearly points to Paul ending his final years in Rome, where he suffered martyrdom under Nero Caesar around 64 A.D.

This outline of Paul's life and mission, as narrated in the Acts of the Apostles, reveals a person dedicated to handing on the gospel of Jesus Christ to the Greek and Roman worlds. This was Paul's total preoccupation: "All this I do for the sake of the gospel, so that I too may have a share in it" (1 Cor 9:23). Paul demonstrates a spiritual vision inspired by a love for and relationship to the Lord. What is so remarkable about Paul's spirituality is his commitment to the Gospel and his willingness to endure every obstacle in the process of handing on the Gospel of Jesus Christ to the peoples of the world. As Paul testifies in his letter to the Philippians,

> . . . I have learned, in whatever situation I find myself, to be self-sufficient. I know indeed how to live in humble circumstances; I know also how to live with abundance. In every circumstance and in all things I have learned the secret of being well fed and of going hungry, of living in abundance and of being in need. I have the strength for everything through him who empowers me. (4:11-13)

Paul's spiritual vision challenges Christians to embrace a similar spirituality that is centered on a relationship with Christ that gives our lives meaning and provides direction and strength amid the vicissitudes of life.

Paul's Call as an Apostle

We return to reflect more fully on Paul's spiritual experience of the risen Jesus that turned his life around and gave him a totally new perspective. Everything that previously had meaning for him now was of little significance, especially his faith as a true Israelite:

> [But] whatever gains I had, these I have come to consider a loss because of Christ. More than that, I even consider everything as a loss because of the supreme good of knowing Christ Jesus my Lord. For his sake I have accepted the loss of all things, and I consider them so much rubbish, that I may gain Christ . . . (Phil 3:7-8)

"That I may gain Christ": Paul's relationship with the risen Christ empowers his entire life. Two different sources in the New Testament give accounts of Paul's total transformation: Luke (in his Acts of the Apostles) and Paul (in his Letter to the Galatians).

Luke's Account (Acts 9:1-19; 22:3-21; and 26:4-23)

Luke's narrative appears on three occasions in the Acts of the Apostles in relatively much the same way (Acts 9:1-19; 22:3-21; and 26:4-23). The first version is narrated in the third person, while the other two are expressed in the first person by Paul. The first version (Acts 9:1-19) is the more extensive account and will be the focus. Told in a very colorful and detailed way, it appeals graphically to the imagination: On the road to Damascus in the early 30s, a dramatic event occurred that made Paul see his life in a new light. Saul (as the text refers to him) experiences a bright light and a voice identifying itself, "I am Jesus, whom you are persecuting . . ." (9:5). Saul loses his sight and is led into Damascus, where a disciple, Ananias (who had received a vision from the Lord), laid his hands on him and said, "Saul, my brother, the Lord has sent me, Jesus who appeared to you on the way by which you came, that you may regain your sight and be filled with the Holy Spirit" (9:17). Scales fall from Saul's eyes and he regains his sight and is baptized. Ananias communicates to Saul the mission that the Lord had given him, "Go, for this man is a chosen instrument of mine to carry my name before Gentiles, kings, and Israelites, and I will show him what he will have to suffer for my name" (Acts 9:15-16).

There is so much local detail in the story (such as the name of Ananias, the name of the street "called Straight," the house of Judas, and Paul's city of origin, Tarsus) that scholars think Luke's account comes from a source in Syria itself.

But, let us not get distracted by all the details of the story. It is the meaning behind this account that is significant.[3] The way the story is told enables the reader to get to the heart of what this experience is about. Saul encounters the risen Jesus as a bright light and in this encounter his life is turned around. He sees and understands things from a new perspective. Saul's physical blindness is a symbol for his interior blindness to the person of Christ that was at the core of his being and how only the light that is Christ could penetrate his depths and transform his life. Saul's response was to accept the gift of the Holy Spirit that Ananias offered and be baptized, enabling the light of Christ to transform his interior darkness so that he could see not just physically but, more importantly, spiritually.

Commenting on this passage, Pope Benedict XVI made an important insight, "In the ancient Church Baptism was also called 'illumination,' because this sacrament gives light; it truly makes one see."[4] As Christians we believe that baptism, as with each of the sacraments, is an encounter with the risen Christ. Paul's encounter was foundational: he experienced the person of Christ in a way that transformed the depths of his being. Paul's conversion did not come as a result of logical arguments or from personal study. His conversion was the result of an encounter with a real person, the risen Jesus.

This event is generally referred to as "Paul's conversion" because his way of living, thinking, and interacting with the world was transformed in a fundamentally different way. But a deeper insight of the nature of this event emerges when we pay close attention to Ananias's declaration to Paul, "This man is a chosen instrument of mine to carry my name before Gentiles, kings, and Israelites, to suffer for my name" (Acts 9:15). God has chosen Paul for a mission: to preach the message of Christ to the nations of the world. Paul received *a call from God that carried with it a mission* in the tradition of the great prophets of the Old Testament (for example, Isa 6:1-10 and Jer 1:4-10). The spiritual implications of this call are significant: his call is not for himself, but for others. While the nature of a conversion looks inward and refers to the individual life, the nature of a call centers on others. Paul is the Lord's instrument to extend belief in Christ Jesus throughout the nations of the world. God is using Paul's gifts, his background, in service to the world. This bears significance for all Christians: baptism in Christ is not only a personal encounter with Christ but brings with it the mission to spread this experience, knowledge, and love of the Lord to others.

Paul's Account (Gal 1:11-24)

Paul narrates his call in the context of his defense of the Gospel he preaches. He refers to his encounter with the risen Lord to avoid the accusation that his message is based upon human sources and hence is unreliable. Paul counters this thought by stating unambiguously that his message comes from God:

> Now I want you to know, brothers, that the gospel preached by me is not of human origin. For I did not receive it from a human being, nor was I taught it, but it came through a revelation of Jesus Christ. . . . But when [God] who from my mother's womb had set me apart and called me through his grace, was pleased to reveal his Son to me, so that I might proclaim him to the Gentiles . . . (Gal 1:12, 15-16)

Paul does not provide a narrative description of the event as Luke does. Paul's life and ministry rested upon God's revelation of the risen Lord. A relationship with Jesus Christ began through this encounter with the risen Christ. One of the major elements of Paul's spirituality is his stress on God's action, not his own. God is in the forefront. Paul contrasts his former way of life to his life now led in Christ (Phil 3:4-11). Formerly, through his own actions, Paul had excelled in his faith "beyond many of my contemporaries among my race" (Gal 1:14) and that led him to persecute Jesus' followers. But God had other plans. Now Paul's life is led in relationship with Christ.

The language of the prophets Isaiah and Jeremiah is clearly in Paul's mind when he speaks of his call through the images of God setting him apart and calling him from his mother's womb for the mission of preaching to the nations:

> Before birth the LORD called me,
>   from my mother's womb he gave me my name. . . .
> I will make you a light to the nations,
>   that my salvation may reach to the ends of the earth.
>   (Isa 49:1, 6)

> Before I formed you in the womb I knew you,
>   before you were born I dedicated you,
>   a prophet to the nations I appointed you. (Jer 1:5)

Two central views are connected: God has called Paul for the purpose of preaching Christ to the nations of the world. As the two prophets Isaiah and Jeremiah demonstrate, God had this plan prior to Paul's conception. The call was not for himself, but for his mission: to preach the message to the nations of the world (the Gentiles). The call is not self-centered but truly "other-centered." Like the prophets, Paul speaks about "the call" God gave him, rather than about a "conversion." His call is for a mission. To prepare him for this mission, God revealed his Son to him (Gal 1:16). Paul is convinced that this Jesus, who was crucified, is now alive. To make sense of this experience, Paul retires into Arabia to reflect alone on his encounter with the risen Lord against the background of his own Israelite faith (1:7). After three years he "went up to Jerusalem to confer with Cephas [Peter] and remained with him for fifteen days. But I did not see any other of the apostles, only James the brother of the Lord" (1:18-19).

Paul alludes to this encounter with the risen Jesus elsewhere on a number of occasions throughout his letters. In discussing the resurrection in 1 Corinthians 15, Paul hands on the tradition about Jesus' resurrection, a tradition that he himself had received, "For I handed on to you as of first importance what I also received . . ." (1 Cor 15:3). This tradition professed the central beliefs of Jesus' followers: he died for our sins as the Hebrew Scriptures had foretold; he was buried and was raised on the third day. As further proof that Jesus was alive, the tradition added that certain witnesses could testify that they had encountered Jesus, such as Peter (Cephas), the Twelve, five hundred believers at the same time, and so on. To this traditional list, Paul adds himself: "Last of all, as to one born abnormally, he appeared to me. For I am the least of the apostles, not fit to be called an apostle, because I persecuted

basic conviction of the Torah (Law) that God promises to the people of Israel that God will never abandon them? Ultimately Paul comes to the conclusion in chapter eleven that although the Gentiles have been grafted onto the olive tree (that is Israel), those dead branches from the olive tree will be grafted back on again (11:24).

The separation between "Judaism" and "Christianity" became a reality only much later, long after Paul's death (ca. AD 64), following the destruction of the temple of Jerusalem (AD 70) and the expulsion of the followers of Jesus from the synagogues (AD 90). Two separate religions emerged from the ashes of the temple and City of Jerusalem.

Illumination: The image the Acts of the Apostles uses of "a light from the sky suddenly flashed around him" (Acts 9:3) helps the reader appreciate the spiritual significance. Light overcomes darkness and makes it possible to see. Light now penetrates the mind of Paul and enables him to see spiritually. Paul's insight in this encounter stems from the grace of the risen Lord. The light of Christ works in his mind and heart enabling him to see with a perspective different from the way he had been able to see previously. Paul, as previously indicated, was steeped in both the traditions of Israel as well as the Hellenistic world. Paul turns the light of Christ onto his own traditions as an Israelite as well as onto the richness of the intellectual world of Rome and Greece. With God's grace he is able to preach his message first to the people of Israel and after that to the Gentiles.

Corporate Unity: Paul realized that in addition to his personal relationship with Christ there is also a bond on a horizontal level with those who believe in Christ, the Body of Christ. His baptism is a sign of his incorporation into the Body of Christ. Aspects of Paul's spiritual and corporate vision are captured so well in the account of Acts. Baptism incorporates the believer into the Body of Christ, and the words of the risen Christ to Paul on the road to Damascus express this bond: "Saul, Saul, why are you persecuting me?" (Acts 9:4). The risen Jesus identifies himself with those whom Paul is persecuting. These powerful words contain an essential awareness of what will become one of Paul's foundational spiritual insights: through faith, baptism, and the gift of the Spirit, the believer is brought into a spiritual bond both with Christ and with all believers. This spiritual bond Paul refers to as "the Body of Christ":

> As a body is one though it has many parts, and all the parts of the body, though many, are one body, so also Christ. For in one Spirit we were all baptized into one body, whether Jews or Greeks, slaves

or free persons, and we were all given to drink of one Spirit. (1 Cor
12:12-13)

Paul's encounter changed his life and influenced the future direction
of early Christianity. Paul's mission was directed to bringing all people
into relationship with Jesus Christ and his message. This became the
foundation for all his missionary journeys. This spiritual vision forms
the core of his life and mission.

Insights for Our Own Spiritual Journey

Encounter–reflection–prolongation is key to every spiritual tradition as
Gutierrez has argued.[5] The same is true of Paul. His spiritual tradition
has been handed down to us in the twenty-first century. What do we
take from Paul's encounter with the risen Christ for our own lives?

Paul's spiritual transformation through an encounter with the risen
Christ is an experience unique to him. Every Christian's journey in life
is different—yet the spiritual elements, significant in Paul's life, are
characteristic of every Christian's spiritual journey: personal experience of Christ; call and mission; illumination; corporate identity. They
are all equally applicable. They are valuable aspects to ponder at the
beginning of our reflection on the meaning of Paul's spirituality for us
in the twenty-first century. These elements give attention to the foundation of the Christian spiritual life.

While very few people will have as dramatic an encounter with the
risen Christ, as both Paul and Luke testify, nevertheless the foundation
and well-spring for our spirituality is always the risen Christ.

A few years ago in a project for a class on Christian Spirituality I
was teaching, the students were assigned to interview people on cam-
pus to find out how they expressed their understanding of spirituality. The students' task was to reflect and comment on these answers
and to draw out their own understanding of spirituality. A couple of
students went to the then president of Gonzaga University, Fr. Robert
Spitzer, SJ,[6] and asked him on camera how he would describe spirituality. Father Spitzer's answer was, "Jesus Christ!" The following silence
lasted about 30 seconds. Obviously, the students recording him were
somewhat taken aback because that was all he said, and they had been
expecting a much longer explanation.

In many ways, this simple yet insightful answer says it all. As Paul
shows us, his Christian journey begins with his encounter with Jesus
Christ, and this Christ remains the center and heart of his whole life,
his spirituality. Christian spirituality has at its root the person of Jesus

Christ who continues to sustain this relationship. Encounter brings with it spiritual transformation.

How do we encounter Christ? Our Christian encounter begins with Baptism. Through Baptism we are born into relationship with Christ and with the Christian community, the Body of Christ. For those baptized as children, it takes time to come to a realization of the full nature of what has happened. For those baptized as adults, there is a unique opportunity of realizing at the beginning of the Christian journey that, like Paul, we are indeed brought into a relationship with the risen Christ—we are "in Christ" who journeys with us throughout our lives. His grace illuminates our paths in relationship to him, to the Body of Christ, and to the world around us. In his letter to the Romans, Paul speaks graphically of our identification with the death and resurrection through baptism:

> Or are you unaware that we who have been baptized into Christ Jesus were baptized into his death? We were indeed buried with him through baptism into death, so that, just as Christ was raised from the dead by the glory of the Father, we too might live in newness of life. (Rom 6:3-4)

Our encounter with Christ continues throughout our Christian lives. We experience Christ in the reading of the Scriptures (the Word of God), in prayer, in the celebration of the sacraments, in the people whom we encounter daily, and in the dwelling presence of Christ within us. At the heart of our Christian life lies this spiritual encounter with Christ. Christianity cannot claim to be only a philosophy, nor simply a morality: at heart it is spirituality, a spiritual relationship with Christ Jesus. This relationship brings us the illumination of Christ's grace that transforms us within and opens us through grace to work toward the transformation of the Body of Christ and of the world.

These spiritual themes of our relationship with Christ and with the Body of Christ identify what is central to Christian spirituality. Our spiritual lives embrace both a vertical direction (our relationship with Christ) and a horizontal direction (our relationship with one another as the Body of Christ). This is significant to realize at the outset of our exploration of Paul's spirituality for often people say all that is necessary is our relationship to Christ. Both are essential because each gives expression to and relies on the other. This vision corresponds to that of Jesus who stressed the commandment of love that embraces both a love for God and a love for our neighbor. Both directions are vital for a full experience of Christian spirituality.

Part Two

Paul's Spiritual Vision

Reflections and Prolongation

The Decisive Significance of the Cross and Resurrection

"And if Christ has not been raised, then empty [too] is our preaching; empty, too, your faith . . . . For if the dead are not raised, neither has Christ been raised, and if Christ has not been raised, your faith is vain; you are still in your sins."
(1 Cor 15:14, 16-17)

As we look back on our life's journey, certain events or experiences stand out as life changing. Such was Paul's encounter with the risen Lord on the road to Damascus. This experience revealed to him the indisputable fact that the Jesus who died on the cross has been raised to life. This encounter shaped the foundation of Paul's faith and the message he preached. By reflecting on his experiences, Paul came to understand that salvation was a gift, a grace that comes to us from the death of Christ. Nothing we do can earn this grace for us. Paul's encounter with the risen Christ transformed his life.

This insight into the free gift of God's grace of salvation triggered an existential revolution in Paul's spiritual thought and life. Paul, like all faithful Israelites, believed that by faithfully carrying out the stipulations of the covenant laws, the people of the covenant earned their salvation. After his experience of the risen Christ, however, Paul realized that the grace of salvation is impossible to attain through one's own efforts. The cross of Christ is the great symbol for God's gift of salvation offered to humanity through his Son. As is evident from Paul's letters, the unifying theme of his spirituality is the cross of salvation, God's greatest gift to his people. As Pope Benedict XVI expressed it: "To say 'Cross' is to say *salvation as grace* given to every creature."[1]

As discussed in the introduction, there comes a time when all people engage what they have inherited from their past and from the world in which they have been raised. Experiences lead people to reassess the values that are important to them. One may reaffirm these values and world perspective or one may come to reject them. In other words, when tradition (the heritage into which one is born) comes into contact with life experience, one is forced to reassess this tradition in light of these experiences. This leads one to appropriate the tradition in a way that gives new insight or meaning. This experience-formed appropriation of tradition gives direction to one's belief system and way of life. Expressed another way, experience enables individuals to internalize their heritage and traditions in a way that gives clear direction to their lives. This is what we term spirituality: one's understanding of God and how that understanding gives direction to one's life.

The same is true of Paul. His encounter with the risen Lord challenged his understanding of his faith tradition, which led him to a deeper insight into his understanding of God as well as humanity's relationship with God and the way of life required by this relationship. As a faithful Jew, Paul embraced the heritage and religion of Israel, including its way of interacting with God and with the world. His worldview and fundamental religious convictions led Paul to reject the concept of a "crucified Messiah" that the early Christians were preaching. Paul was convinced of his understanding of his heritage and the way of life he was called to lead. All this changed through his encounter with the risen Lord.

Paul's Spiritual Insight into the Significance of the Cross

As a dedicated Pharisee, Paul could not understand how this Jesus who was crucified could be acknowledged as the long-awaited Messiah. On the basis of their heritage, traditions, and understanding of their sacred writings, many of the people of Israel believed the long-awaited Messiah would come as a king, a descendant from the line of David, to establish God's kingdom. Just as David's rule was viewed as "a golden age," the people of Israel believed firmly that God would recreate this kingdom and rule over them once again. This belief was founded upon God's promise to King David when he wanted to build a house to contain the Ark of the Covenant. Instead of a physical house, God promises that King David's lineage (his house) will continue forever:

> Moreover, the LORD also declares to you that the LORD will make a house for you: when your days have been completed and you rest with your ancestors, I will raise up your offspring after you, sprung from your loins, and I will establish his kingdom . . . Your house and your kingdom are firm forever before me; your throne shall be firmly established forever. (2 Sam 7:11b-12, 16)

This hope continued to inspire the people of Israel, especially throughout those centuries when their kingdom had been destroyed. Psalm 89 expresses this same hope:

> I myself make him the firstborn,
>> Most High over the kings of the earth.
> Forever I will maintain my mercy for him;
>> my covenant with him stands firm.
> I will establish his dynasty forever;
>> his throne as the days of the heavens. (Ps 89:28-30)

In addition to this hope for the reestablishment of God's kingdom over Israel, another aspect troubled Paul. In his letter to the Galatians, Paul quotes the saying of Deuteronomy 21:23, "Cursed be everyone who hangs upon a tree" (Gal 3:13). In effect, Paul, the Pharisee, interpreted the curse in this way: "How could this person, Jesus, crucified as a common criminal, be proclaimed to be the Messiah? By being raised upon the cross, Jesus bore upon himself the curse contained in the Book of Deuteronomy!" Since Paul was convinced the followers of the crucified Jesus were distorting the traditional beliefs of the people of Israel, he opposed them vehemently.

Paul's encounter with the risen Lord on the road to Damascus changed his theological outlook radically. His experience convinced him that this Jesus, who had been put to death, was now alive. Following this encounter, Paul went into the desert of Arabia for three years (Gal 1:15-18) to reflect more deeply on its significance. Faced with the certainty of his own experience, Paul returned to his traditions, to the Sacred Scriptures, to understand how these two seemingly inconsistent ideas could be reconciled. Paul discovered another theme running through the Sacred Scriptures, namely the theme of the Suffering Servant. Isaiah 52:13–53:12 speaks of a suffering servant who dies on behalf of the sins of all people. This text read like a blueprint for the ministry of Jesus. Paul interpreted the servant as referring to Jesus and came to understand that God's curse (in Deut 21:23) was intended not for Jesus but for us. This insight gave rise to an understanding within the traditions of Christianity that on the cross Jesus bore the sins of humanity.

The resurrection of Jesus was God's supreme act by which God showed acceptance of the life and obedience of Jesus by raising him from the dead. Ultimately, Paul's experience helped him understand his traditions in a new light. Focusing on the tradition of the Suffering Servant as foreshadowing the person of Jesus, Paul understood

Jesus' suffering as a participation in God's plan where suffering has a redemptive value. The crucifixion of Jesus demonstrated that the kingdom God promised to David was a spiritual kingdom where people entered into a close personal relationship with the God of the covenant. While the tradition of God's promises to David had been read in a political sense, Paul understood that this was not God's intent—God was to establish a spiritual relationship through his Son with humanity.

The Paradox of the Cross

In the opening chapters of the first letter to the Corinthians, Paul reflects further upon the cross of Jesus and sees it as a stumbling block for both the people of Israel and those in the Greco-Roman world:

> The message of the cross is foolishness to those who are perishing, but to us who are being saved it is the power of God . . . For Jews demand signs and Greeks look for wisdom, but we proclaim Christ crucified, a stumbling block to Jews and foolishness to Gentiles, but to those who are called, Jews and Greeks alike, Christ the power of God and the wisdom of God. For the foolishness of God is wiser than human wisdom, and the weakness of God is stronger than human strength. (1 Cor 1:18, 22-25)

For the people of Israel, the cross was a *skandalon* (a snare or stumbling block). In the preaching of the apostles, the message of the cross becomes, as it were, an obstacle that "causes offense or revulsion and results in opposition, disapproval, or hostility."[2] Why should the message of the cross be a stumbling block for the people of Israel? For Paul the reason was clear: the message of the cross challenged their faith. They had failed to notice the significance of the cross and suffering in their Sacred Scriptures. In their minds, the idea of God being powerless, as seen in Christ on the cross, ran counter to God's very nature. Throughout their history and in the course of their sacred writings, God always demonstrated power through mighty works of salvation. The crucified Jesus was exactly the opposite: a demonstration of powerlessness.

The Greeks, or Gentiles (meaning "nations" and referring to non-Jews), rejected the cross on the basis of their natural desire for wisdom based on human reason. They judged the message of the cross and resurrection to be pure folly (*mōría*)—it defied every form of logic and practical judgment. Paul's sermon in Athens during his second missionary journey (Acts 17:22-34) illustrates well how the Athenians rejected his message of the cross and resurrection as unworthy of being taken seriously. At the end of the sermon, when Paul spoke about Jesus being raised from the dead, Luke described the reaction of the Athenian listeners in this way, "When they heard about resurrection of the dead, some began to scoff, but others said, 'We should like to hear you on this some other time'" (Acts 17:32). Paul's words fell on deaf ears— his message was not to be taken seriously.

Contrasted to the people of Israel who saw the cross as a stumbling block and the Greeks who saw it as pure foolishness, Paul sees it as a demonstration of God's power: "The message of the cross is foolishness to those who are perishing, but to us who are being saved it is the power of God" (1 Cor 1:18). Herein rests a paradox: in the weakness of the cross, the power of God is displayed.

The Paradox of Weakness

The foundation of Paul's preaching about the cross rests on his own experience that in weakness the "power of God" is experienced; "For the foolishness of God is wiser than human wisdom, and the weakness of God is stronger than human strength" (1 Cor 1:25). When Paul experienced his own weakness he experienced more fully God's power. But what exactly is understood by this power? Paul uses it in reference to the cross to say, in the words of Graham Tomlin, that power "is the capability to influence people or situations and *to transform them.*"[3] By raising Jesus from the dead, God transforms the weakness of the cross. The resurrection brings about the promise of transformation for all who believe in Jesus as the Christ. Paul's expression of the Gospel message is outlined succinctly in what has been termed "his thesis statement"[4] for the letter to the Romans:

> For I am not ashamed of the gospel. It is the power of God for the salvation of everyone who believes; for Jew first, and then Greek. For in it is revealed the righteousness of God from faith to faith; as it is written, "The one who is righteous by faith will live." (Rom 1:16-17)

As God's word, the Gospel message is not simply the content that is communicated. According to the understanding of the Old Testament, God's word always has the power to transform, to accomplish what God intends:

> Yet just as from the heavens
> > the rain and the snow come down

And do not return there
till they have watered the earth
making it fertile and fruitful . . .
So shall my word be
that goes forth from my mouth;
It shall not return to me empty,
but shall do what pleases me,
achieving the end for which I sent it. (Isa 55:10-11)

The paradox of weakness becomes explicit here. On the cross Jesus is publicly displayed as a common criminal subject to human power and the forces of evil. In the midst of such weakness, the true power of God emerges. The cross points to its significance: a sacrifice for the sins of humanity. Not only does it proclaim this fact, but it also accomplishes it. By his death we are healed. As the prophet Isaiah proclaimed centuries before Jesus,

Yet it was our pain that he bore,
our sufferings he endured.
We thought of him as stricken,
struck down by God and afflicted,
But he was pierced for our sins,
crushed for our iniquity.
He bore the punishment that makes us whole,
by his wounds we were healed. (Isa 53:4-5)

Jesus' death on the cross brings with it forgiveness for the sins of humanity and reconciliation with God. Paul explains that this forgiveness liberates humanity from the powers that enslave them (sin, death, and the law) and communicates God's grace, the gift of eternal life:

For just as through the disobedience of one person the many were made sinners, so through the obedience of one the many will be made righteous. The law entered in so that transgression might increase but, where sin increased, grace overflowed all the more, so that, as sin reigned in death, grace also might reign through justification for eternal life through Jesus Christ our Lord. (Rom 5:19-21)

In his own human weakness, Paul also experienced God's transforming power at work in him:

About myself I will not boast, except about my weaknesses . . . that I may not become too elated, a thorn in the flesh was given to me, an angel of Satan, to beat me, to keep me from being too elated. Three times I begged the Lord about this, that it might leave, but he

said to me, "My grace is sufficient for you, for power is made perfect in weakness." I will rather boast most gladly of my weaknesses,
in order that the power of Christ may dwell with me. Therefore, I
am content with weaknesses, insults, hardships, persecutions, and
constraints, for the sake of Christ; for when I am weak, then I am
strong. (2 Cor 12:5, 7b-10)

This autobiographical piece gives insight into the essence of Paul's
spirituality. Just as the weakness of the cross displays God's power
at work, the weakness in Paul's own life experiences God's power of
transformation. When Paul first came to Corinth and preached there,
he was aware of his own inability: he came to them "in weakness and
fear and much trembling" (1 Cor 2:3). His life emulates the same mystery of the cross. Not only is it a spiritual identification with the cross of
Christ but also a bodily identification. God's transforming grace works
through Paul to accomplish its purpose in the lives of those Corinthians who heard Paul's message.

In 2 Corinthians 5:13-21 Paul expresses the essence of his understanding of the cross in this way: "He indeed died for all, so that those
who live might no longer live for themselves but for him who for their
sake died and was raised" (2 Cor 5:15). The implications are clear: let
go of dependence upon ourselves and our own power and rely upon
God's power. Like Paul, the foundation of our spirituality rests on embracing God's power and acknowledging our own weakness by embracing a life of humility where love guides our every action.

The Decisive Event: The Resurrection

Paul offers no description of Jesus' crucifixion, death, and resurrection in his letters. The focus of his spirituality rests not on the narrative but on the spiritual significance of the connection of the cross
and the resurrection. Whenever Paul speaks of the cross in his letters,
he always connects it with the resurrection of Jesus. In 1 Corinthians
15:1-58 Paul addresses belief in the resurrection to resolve certain problems that had arisen in the community regarding the resurrection. Paul
begins by reminding them of the Gospel he had preached to them:
"For I handed on to you as of first importance what I also received:
that Christ died for our sins in accordance with the scriptures; that he
was buried; that he was raised on the third day in accordance with the
scriptures; that he appeared to Cephas . . ." (15:3-5). Tradition testified that Jesus died and was raised. Proof comes from the testimony of
so many eyewitnesses. For Paul, the fact of the resurrection lies at the

heart of the faith of Christianity: without the resurrection, the cross is meaningless. Without the resurrection there is also no salvation. Paul's foundational belief would also be an illusion: faith would not result in justification or salvation:

> And if Christ has not been raised, then empty [too] is our preaching; empty, too, your faith . . . For if the dead are not raised, neither has Christ been raised, and if Christ has not been raised, your faith is vain; you are still in your sins. (1 Cor 15:14, 16-17)

Without the risen Christ, the cross made no sense. The foundation for belief in Jesus' resurrection rested upon Jesus' appearances to Paul and the other disciples. Paul offers a list of those who had encountered the risen Christ:

> . . . he appeared to Cephas, then to the Twelve. After that, he appeared to more than five hundred brothers at once, most of whom are still living, though some have fallen asleep. After that he appeared to James, then to all the apostles. Last of all, as to one born abnormally, he appeared to me . . . (1 Cor 15:5-8)

This list of appearances is not meant to be all inclusive. The gospels mention other appearances. Of importance is the confession that "for many days he appeared to those who had come up with him from Galilee to Jerusalem" (Acts 13:31). The major difference between Paul's tradition and the gospel tradition is that Paul makes no mention of the empty tomb. Paul has based his testimony on a traditional formula he had received and was not, like the gospels, giving a narrative account of the events surrounding the resurrection of Jesus.

In reflecting on the resurrection of Jesus, Paul goes further to explore its implications for believers in the present and in the future. Its significance for the present occurs in baptism where the baptismal ritual enables an encounter with the death and resurrection of Christ: "We were indeed buried with him through baptism into death, so that, just as Christ was raised from the dead by the glory of the Father, we too might live in newness of life" (Rom 6:4). By being baptized into the death and resurrection of Christ, the Christian participates in Christ's death and resurrection.

Jesus' resurrection also bears a *future significance* for all believers: "But now Christ has been raised from the dead, the firstfruits of those who have fallen asleep" (1 Cor 15:20). As the firstfruits, Jesus guarantees the future resurrection for his followers. Paul's reflections draw out the sig-

nificance of the death-resurrection of Christ for the Corinthians and ultimately for Christians today. His discussion focuses on objections to the
idea of the resurrection of the dead that he faced coming from two different sources: the Greeks and the people of Israel.

The great Greek philosopher Plato had taught that the body was the
prison house of the soul. Death would liberate the soul from its imprisonment within the body. The idea that the human person would
continue to live in the future as body and soul was seen as illogical to
the Greeks. Paul countered their idea by upholding the connection between soul and body and explaining that while the body, being material, would die, the future body becomes a transformed spiritual body.
To illustrate his belief, Paul uses the image of a seed that is sown in the
ground. "What you sow is not brought to life unless it dies" (15:36).
Like a seed, the body dies, is placed in the ground, and then is raised,
transformed, and adapted to the spiritual world by God: "So also is the
resurrection of the dead. It is sown corruptible; it is raised incorrupt-
ible. It is sown dishonorable; it is raised glorious. It is sown weak; it is
raised powerful. It is sown a natural body; it is raised a spiritual body.
If there is a natural body, there is also a spiritual one" (15:42-44).

Paul also addresses objections from the people of Israel, some of
whom had a too-literal, materialistic interpretation of what the resurrected body would be like. For Paul, in the resurrection of the dead, the
body is transformed to suit the spiritual world. The physical body is
transformed into a spiritual body, "And when this which is corruptible
clothes itself with immortality, and this which is mortal clothes itself
with immortality" (1 Cor 15:54).

Insights for Our Own Spiritual Journey: Spiritual Response to the Cross and Resurrection Today

Spirituality of Humility

The resurrection reveals the true identity of Jesus, the crucified one.
In beginning his letter to the Romans, Paul writes that the Gospel is
"about his Son, descended from David according to the flesh, but established as Son of God in power . . ." (Rom 1:3-4). From his birth, Jesus
is Son of God in the weakness of his human existence; now through
the resurrection from the dead he is established as Son of God in the
fullness of God's power. In the resurrection, the Son of God is revealed
in all his glory in his relationship with the Father. In the resurrection,
he is also acknowledged to be in relationship with us as "our Lord"
(Rom 1:4).

Paul proclaims the same understanding about the identity of Jesus Christ (as seen in his incarnation and resurrection) in his letter to the Philippians. In Philippians 2:5-11, Paul has left us one of the most poetic passages of the New Testament. Probably it originated as an ancient Christian hymn sung in honor of Christ Jesus when Christians gathered in worship. Paul adapted this hymn to illustrate how Christians should follow the example of Christ. The New Testament refers to Christians as "singing hymns to God" (see Acts 16:25). Even some pagan writers, such as Pliny the Younger, referred to Christians as singing "a hymn to Christ as to a god" (*Letter 10 to Trajan*, 10.96-97, written around AD 110).

> [Christ Jesus] though he was in the form of God,
>> did not regard equality with God something to be grasped.
>> Rather, he emptied himself,
>> taking the form of a slave,
>> coming in human likeness;
>> and found human in appearance,
>> he humbled himself,
>>> becoming obedient to death,
>>> even death on a cross.
> Because of this, God greatly exalted him
>> and bestowed on him the name
>> that is above every name,
>> that at the name of Jesus
>> every knee should bend,
>> of those in heaven and on earth and under the earth,
>> and every tongue confess that
>> Jesus Christ is Lord,
>> to the glory of God the Father. (Phil 2:5-11)

Scholars refer to this hymn as the *"kenotic hymn"* (*kenōsis* is a Greek word that means "emptying") because it expresses how Jesus left aside aspects of his divinity to take on the weakness of our human nature. The hymn is a beautiful expression of the whole mystery of Jesus' life from his preexistence through his incarnation to his passion and resurrection. His incarnation embraces the weakness and lowliness of the human condition in obedience to the will of the Father. By entering into the human condition, Jesus also accepted death as central to what it means to be human (2:8). However, his death went beyond anything that most humans experience. He embraced an ignominious death as a common criminal on a cross. The second part of the hymn (2:9-11) shows the Father responding to Jesus' obedience by raising him from the dead and exalting him to his right hand. The whole universe now worships him ("every knee should bend") and acknowledges him as "Lord." The title "Lord" was the Old Testament way of referring to God. This proclamation of Jesus as "Lord" by all creation effectively acknowledged his equality with God.

In this hymn, Paul illustrates beautifully the very nature of spirituality. His purpose in using this hymn in his letter was not to offer a theological teaching for his readers on the ontology of Jesus Christ. Instead he presents this hymn as a call on his readers to respond by their way of life to this understanding of the person of Jesus Christ. As indicated throughout, Christian spirituality is a response made to the understanding of God as seen in the person of Jesus Christ. In effect, Paul states: "This is who Jesus is in relationship to the Father and to us. Consequently, you (Christians) should emulate Jesus' way of acting." Although equal to the Father, Jesus embraced lowliness and humility in order to accomplish the Father's will. Like Jesus, we too are called to embrace a life of humility in which we acknowledge that we too are "slaves" (servants) in our relationship to God. As the life of Jesus embraced an obedience that led to death on a cross, so our lives should embrace obedience to the Father's will for us. As with Jesus' life, so too our lives will involve suffering as part of the human condition. As the Father responded to his obedience by exalting him through the resurrection, so our lives lead through obedience to the resurrection. By leading lives in service and fidelity to the Father's will, we will experience the fullness of life in the exaltation of the resurrection. The life of Jesus bears witness to the ultimate expression of what Christian spirituality involves: fidelity to the will of the Father through a life of humility and suffering that leads to the resurrection.

Spirituality Embracing the Death and Resurrection of Christ

Humility is the virtue that embraces our identity as humans in relationship to God our Father and Creator. Humility also includes our identity in relationship to others. As brothers and sisters in Christ, we take on the same attitude Paul identifies in Philippians 2:5. Christians are called to serve their brothers and sisters through suffering and even laying down their lives for them, just as Jesus did for all humanity. Paul's whole life was one of service and concern for the communities he had established. This is seen in the reflection offered in this verse: "Now I rejoice in my sufferings for your sake, and in my flesh I am filling up what is lacking in the afflictions of Christ on behalf of his body" (Col 1:24). This passage comes from a disciple of Paul writing after Paul's death and is a reflection on how Paul is being perceived within the context of the early Christian community toward the end of the first century AD.

While this is a difficult passage to interpret, a number of things are clear. It is beyond dispute that there is nothing lacking in the sufferings of Christ who obtained salvation for all through his death on the cross. He atoned for the sin of Adam and the sins of humanity as Paul describes, "He delivered us from the power of darkness and transferred us to the kingdom of his beloved Son, in whom we have redemption, the forgiveness of sins" (Col 1:13-14).

On the other hand, as the Body of Christ, we are all united with one another. The sufferings that each member of this body endures have an influence on all members of this body. Paul learned this foundational belief when he met the risen Christ on the road to Damascus: "Saul, Saul, why are you persecuting me?" (Acts 9:4). This experience generated Paul's understanding of the Body of Christ, our union with Christ. Consequently, we influence one another's lives. The suffering of one is experienced as a suffering of all. Vincent M. Smiles offers an insightful interpretation of "what is lacking in the afflictions of Christ" (Col 1:24):

> Dwelling on Paul's thoughts about his sufferings as an apostle (especially 2 Cor 4:7-10), the writer sees them as having a role "for your sake . . . on behalf of [Christ's] body, the church" . . . It might be, as one author has suggested, that the crucial phrase should be hyphenated, "I am completing what is lacking in *Christ's-afflictions-in-my-flesh* for the sake of his body." In this case, it is not Christ's own sufferings that might be lacking, but rather the sufferings of Paul for the sake of Christ and the church.[5]

Like the head, the body also has to suffer. The sufferings of the body of Christ are a way of experiencing the same path as Jesus that moved from suffering through death to the resurrection. Paul speaks to the Romans as "heirs of God and joint heirs with Christ, if only we suffer with him so that we may also be glorified with him" (Rom 8:17). In embracing suffering in this manner, the believer is imitating the path of Jesus Christ. The work of Christ continues in the world today. The suffering of the Body of Christ continues throughout history. Paul unites himself with these sufferings as does every Christian as a member of the body of Christ: "If [one] part suffers, all the parts suffer with it; if one part is honored, all the parts share its joy" (1 Cor 12:26).

Spirituality that Hands on the Tradition Faithfully

"By the grace of God I am what I am, and his grace to me has not been ineffective. Indeed, I have toiled harder than all of them; not I, however, but the grace of God [that is] with me. Therefore, whether it be I or they, so we preach and so you believed" (1 Cor 15:10-11). Here Paul is speaking of himself and the other apostles. Paul's belief in the resurrection rests on his own encounter with the risen Christ. The same is true of those first followers whose faith also rested upon their encounters with the risen Jesus shortly after his death (1 Cor 15:5-6). Paul based his understanding of the encounters of the other apostles on the tradition that he himself had received (1 Cor 15:3). Paul shows here an essential aspect regarding passing on the message of Christ Jesus. Paul is a significant link in the chain of tradition that goes back from the apostles to Jesus. He remains true to this tradition and hands it on to his communities as faithfully as possible. Paul's communities take on a new role in that they now become links in the chain of faith and tradition. Today, through our faith, we are true to this rich two-thousand-year tradition. Like Paul, ours is the task of faithfully transmitting this tradition to a future generation. Pope Benedict XVI drew attention to how Paul's transmission of the tradition offers a paradigm for the way theologians and preachers should work:

> In this way, Saint Paul offers a model for all time of how to approach theology and how to preach. The theologian, the preacher, does not create new visions of the world and of life, but he [*sic*] is at the service of truth handed down, at the service of the real fact of Christ, of the cross and of the resurrection.[6]

We hand on the teaching that has been received. Naturally we try to hand on the message in ways our generation understands. Paul's speech to the Athenians at the Areopagus gives us a beautiful insight into how Paul used the language and philosophy of his audience to preach the gospel message of salvation:

> I even discovered an altar inscribed, "To an Unknown God." What therefore you unknowingly worship, I proclaim to you . . . For "In him we live and move and have our being," as even some of your poets have said, "For we too are his offspring." (Acts 17:23, 28)

Despite using the language and thought patterns of his audience, Paul remained true to the message he had received. To them he preached the message of the resurrection of Christ Jesus from the dead, a message they could not accept given their own philosophical views concerning the immortality of the soul.

A living tradition continues to gain insight into the truth of the message that has been handed down over the centuries. We do not rely on our own views and ideas, but we remain true to the tradition that has been passed on to us by our faith community. Our task, just as it was Paul's, is to hand on what we have received.

God's Transforming Grace

"But he said to me, 'My grace is sufficient for you, for power is made perfect in weakness.' . . . Therefore, I am content with weaknesses, insults, hardships, persecutions, and constraints, for the sake of Christ; for when I am weak, then I am strong."

(2 Cor 12:9-10)

Paul views his foundational encounter with the risen Lord in terms of a call that transformed his life from an unworthy recipient into an apostle to the nations. Nothing he had done had brought this about—it was pure gift. For Paul, all is grace, all is God's gift. Paul describes his call in terms of an act of God's grace: "But when [God], who from my mother's womb had set me apart and called me through his grace, was pleased to reveal his Son to me . . ." (Gal 1:15-16). The word "grace" (in Greek, "*charis*," from which we derive the English words "*charismatic*" and "*charism*") refers in this passage to God as the source of every blessing given to humanity.

The importance of God's grace for Paul's spiritual thought emerges in the opening of every one of his letters. He greets his readers with a blessing, "Grace to you and peace from God our Father and the Lord Jesus Christ" (see Rom 1:7 and 1 Cor 1:3).[1] Using the opening formula of a Greek letter, Paul adapts it in two meaningful ways. Instead of the word "greetings" (in Greek, *charein*), Paul uses a closely connected word "grace" (*charis*). To this Paul adds the word "peace" that is a reminder of the Hebrew greeting *shalom*. Paul has deliberately chosen to combine two greetings in order to embrace his readers, who came from different backgrounds (from the worlds of Greece-Rome and from Israel). This is Paul's unique way of uniting his readers in the one faith no matter their background. Paul goes even further in his greeting by transforming it into a blessing that comes from "God our Father and the Lord Jesus Christ." God is the source of every blessing and peace that comes down upon believers. Paul often ends his letters with a further blessing that invokes God's grace on his readers, "The grace of the Lord Jesus be with you" (1 Cor 16:23). Like bookends for his letters, Paul calls down the blessing of God's grace upon his readers. It is within this context that his words within the letters are to be understood.

Centrality of Grace in Paul's Spiritual Life

Paul uses the term "grace" (*charis*) in his writings in two ways, yet both are intimately connected. On the one hand, Paul views grace from the perspective of God as the source and origin of every blessing. On the other hand, Paul considers grace from the perspective of the believer who receives God's blessings. These two perspectives demonstrate the richness of this concept. Grace is like a coin that can be viewed on the obverse side as God, the source, who bestows blessings on humanity, while on the reverse side as the blessings themselves that the human person receives.

Grace as God's Divine Help

Grace is considered from the perspective of the recipient, the human person, who receives God's blessings. Grace is most often experienced as the help God pours forth on believers to enable them to live faithfully as followers of Christ and to accomplish the tasks the Lord has assigned them. Paul refers to his ministry as "the grace of apostleship" (Rom 1:5).

For Paul, this grace is the source of everything he does: "But by the grace of God I am what I am, and his grace to me has not been ineffective. Indeed, I have toiled harder than all of them; not I, however, but the grace of God [that is] with me" (1 Cor 15:10). God's grace empowers him throughout his ministry and in all his activity. God's grace has transformed Paul while at the same time calling forth from Paul a response to this grace that has been given him. In writing to the Corinthians, Paul reflects on how he has led his life in obedience to the grace God has given him, "For our boast is this, the testimony of our conscience that we have conducted ourselves in the world, and especially toward you, with the simplicity and sincerity of God, [and] not by human wisdom but by the grace of God" (2 Cor 1:12).

In the lives of his communities, Paul also sees how they have been responding to God's grace empowering their concern for others. For example, in 2 Corinthians 8:1–9:15, Paul speaks about the collection he was taking up among the churches in Macedonia for the poor in Jerusalem as he had been asked to do by the Council of Jerusalem (Gal 2:10). God's grace had enabled the Macedonians to respond generously (2 Cor 8:1).

Grace as God's Saving Will in Christ

In Paul's writings, grace is often understood within the framework of God's work of salvation. God is the source and origin of grace. As the *Anchor Bible Dictionary* expresses it, "Grace frequently denotes God's giving of himself in Christ in or to effect salvation for the undeserving."[2] For Paul, a right relationship with God is only possible through God's grace: "All have sinned and are deprived of the glory of God. They are justified freely by his grace through the redemption in Christ Jesus" (Rom 3:23-24). Paul does not reflect upon the nature of God as a gracious God. Rather, his focus is on the actual experience and making God's grace known and realized in the crucifixion of Christ: "I have been crucified with Christ; yet I live, no longer I, but Christ lives in me; insofar as I now live in the flesh, I live by faith in the Son of God who has loved me and given himself up for me. I do not nullify the grace of God; for if justification comes through the law, then Christ died for nothing" (Gal 2:19-21). These words capture beautifully Paul's whole spirituality. When we are baptized we are baptized into Christ, into his crucifixion and death (as Paul says in Rom 6:6). Having died in Christ, we now live through his saving grace. We are saved by grace that comes to us through the cross of Christ.

Perhaps the most distinctive feature of Paul's understanding of grace is the totally free and gratuitous nature of this gift of God. Salvation is not earned ourselves, but is freely given by God. It shows the absolute generosity of God as Father who gave his only Son to bring us back into relationship with him. "If God is for us, who can be against us? He who did not spare his own Son but handed him over for us all, how will he not also give us everything else along with him?" (Rom 8:31-32). Faith that comes to us through the grace of God enables us to recognize this wonderful nature of God's gracious saving will and saving actions in Christ.

Understanding the Relationship Initiated by God's Grace

In order to understand more clearly this twofold idea of grace in Paul's writings, one must consider the foundations for this view of grace within the cultural and social world of the New Testament. In the cultural world of the Mediterranean, grace is a concept that captures the foundational relationships among human beings as well as between humans and the divine world. In the Old Testament, the words *ḥen* (grace, favor) and *ḥesed* (covenant love, steadfast love) are used to express God's favor toward humanity and God's loyalty to those who accept God's favor. The well-known phrase, "find grace, find favor in the sight of God" captures well this concept of the positive attitude of one freely acting with kindness toward another and the joyous expression on the face of the person who bestows the favor. The beautiful blessing in the book of Numbers captures this idea well:

> The LORD bless you and keep you!
> The LORD let his face shine upon you, and be gracious to you!
> The LORD look upon you kindly and give you peace!
>   (Num 6:24-26)

The Psalms at their very heart attempt to express the relationship between God and the people of Israel. The people often call upon God to turn a happy face toward them and grant the petitioners God's kindness and favor:

> Turn to me, be gracious to me;
>   give your strength to your servant;
>   save the son of your handmaid. (Ps 86:16)

The divine-human relationship is expressed in terms of time and reflects the way in which human beings interacted with one another. People who were in a lower position in society would turn to those who were in a superior position to solicit their help. The story of Joseph in the house of Potiphar (Gen 39:4, 31; 50:4) is a good illustration of this interchange where an inferior person is supported by a superior figure. Such was the case of Joseph, who received the favor of Potiphar as well as the jailor.

The covenant relationship between God and the people of Israel forms the basis for God's free action on behalf of God's people. Nothing the people of Israel do or have done can earn this favorable action: it is totally undeserved. Even when they sinned and turned away from the stipulations of the covenant, God's love for them never changed. We can perhaps express this action as "grace": God's free and undeserved response when an appeal is made to God for God's help by an individual or a group in need.

In the New Testament world, the Good News of God's free gift of salvation in his Son Jesus would have been understood in terms of the role patronage played as the glue that held the society together and was at the heart of all relationships.[3] The Roman Stoic philosopher and statesman Seneca (4 BC–65 AD) referred to the role patronage played as "the chief bond of human society."[4] The frequently used phrase in the

Old Testament, "If I find favor with you [literally, 'in your eyes'], Lord" (Exod 34:9), actually expressed what the Roman-Greek world understood about a patron who bestowed blessings on his clients. The word "patron" comes from the Greek and Latin words for "father" (*pater*). In fact, when the Bible calls someone "father" who is not the biological father, the concept of patronage comes into play. When Jesus refers to God as "Father," he is using the terms of kinship to express what the world of his time would clearly understand as a "patron-client relationship." Patrons supported their clients with the necessary means for their livelihood, protection, and promotion. On the other side, clients would show loyalty to their patron and would contribute to the honor of their patron's name. The client would relate to the patron in the same way the child would relate to the parent, just as the patron would relate to the client as parent to child.[5]

Between these two roles of patron and client was a third role, that of a broker whose task it was to act as a patron to his own clients while at the same time being a client to another more influential and powerful patron. This "Patron—Broker—Client" model was at the heart of all relationships in the first few centuries around the Christian era. It was also at the heart of the relationships that were established between God, Christ, and the believer. As the Patron, God is completely free in offering salvation to all peoples. God is the one who inspired Paul to reach out on his missionary journeys to the Gentiles, the people of the world. In terms of these relationships, Paul's message of God's free gift of salvation would have been understood. In turn, the believers (in the role of clients) have the obligation to respond with sincerity, loyalty, and obedience. "Everything indeed is for you, so that the grace bestowed in abundance on more and more people may cause the thanksgiving to overflow for the glory of God" (2 Cor 4:15). This has serious implications for believers: to continue to rely upon the law as the means of remaining in this patronage relationship is in effect a rejection of the role Jesus Christ plays as the broker between God and believers. Reliance upon the law is a demonstration that they are relying upon their own efforts to maintain this relationship with God. But their own efforts are not enough to maintain loyalty to the God who has given them so freely this covenant relationship. The only way in which this covenantal relationship can be maintained is through the grace of salvation that comes to them through the broker, Jesus Christ: "I do not nullify the grace of God; for if justification comes through the law then Christ died for nothing" (Gal 2:21).[6]

By returning to a reliance upon their own works in carrying out the law, the believers would show that they had rejected Christ and were relying upon themselves. The role that Jesus, as broker, plays in the drama of salvation would be nullified, as Paul says in Gal 2:21. Through his death on the cross, Jesus (as *broker*) is the agent of God the Father (as *patron*) to bring together Jews and Gentiles (the *clients*) into a relationship with God. This gift, "salvation of grace," is offered to humanity through Jesus, and human beings respond to this tremendous offer of grace by their "obedience of faith." "Through him [Jesus Christ our Lord] we have received the grace of apostleship, to bring about the obedience of faith, for the sake of his name, among all the Gentiles" (Rom 1:5).

Partners with Paul in Grace

In Paul's spirituality the word "grace" encapsulates the very heart of his spiritual thought and legacy. Jesus Christ, in his obedience to his Father, is the ultimate self-giving for the sake of the salvation of all humanity. In Romans 5:12-21, Paul compares the entry of sin into the world through Adam's rejection of God to the coming of grace through the obedience of the person Jesus Christ. "For if by that one person's transgression the many died, how much more did the grace of God and the gracious gift of the one person Jesus Christ overflow for the many" (Rom 5:15). While Adam transgressed and rejected his relationship with God, affecting the whole human race, the obedience of Jesus to his Father's will brings the grace of salvation to all people. This gift of grace establishes not only a vertical relationship between God and the individual believer but also a horizontal relationship. Grace comes in Christ, and to continue to live in Christ requires that one lives in grace as a fellow member of the Body of Christ. Paul expresses this notion of our unity with one another so beautifully in the letter to the Philippians—where Paul, despite being in prison, shows his continued union with the believers in Philippi, "It is right that I should think this way about all of you, because I hold you in my heart, you who are all partners with me in grace" (Phil 1:7). What a wonderful phrase, "partners with Paul in grace!"

Transformative Power of Grace

Throughout his life Paul shows God's grace at work transforming him. Nowhere is this more evident than in his weakness and in his suffering. Just as God's grace is made effective in the suffering and crucifixion of Jesus, so too God's grace transforms Paul's own sufferings and weakness into an identification with the suffering and dying Christ. God's grace is a power transforming Paul, giving him the strength to endure his weaknesses and sufferings. On his own, he could not do it. Grace empowers Paul spiritually.

A Spirituality that Discovers the Redemptive Power of Suffering

For Paul, suffering and the cross are not ends in themselves. When Paul addresses suffering as a union with the suffering of the cross of Christ, he situates it within a specific context. Suffering is not sought for its own sake. Paul does not embrace a "masochistic" attitude toward suffering. The sufferings Paul speaks about are those that come in the course of life, whether physical or spiritual. The positive value of suffering emerges in its identification with the spiritual meaning of the cross of Christ.

In human weakness, God's power is most clearly evident. Throughout his life, Paul experienced God's power transforming his human weakness. Nowhere is this more evident than in Paul's reflection on his own experiences, as recorded in 2 Corinthians 11:21b–12:10. The context of this passage within his letter to the Corinthians illustrates clearly Paul's aim. In Corinth, Paul's opponents have so impressed the Corinthians by boasting about their accomplishments and abilities that they have, as it were, "seduced" the Corinthians into accepting their false teaching. In his turn, Paul boasts, but he does so sarcastically, of his weakness:

> But he said to me, "My grace is sufficient for you, for power is made perfect in weakness." I will rather boast most gladly of my weaknesses, in order that the power of Christ may dwell with me. Therefore, I am content with weaknesses, insults, hardships, persecutions, and constraints, for the sake of Christ; for when I am weak, then I am strong. (2 Cor 12:9-10)

Paul's Weakness Displayed in Personal Presence and Lack of Rhetorical Skills

Paul's opponents in Corinth ridiculed him for his lack of personal appeal. According to Paul, they claimed that "his letters are severe and forceful, but his bodily presence is weak, and his speech is contemptible" (2 Cor 10:10). Even the apocryphal book from the second century, Acts of Paul and Thecla 3, describes Paul in an unassuming way as "a man small of stature, with a bald head and crooked legs, in a good state of body, with eyebrows meeting and nose somewhat hooked, full of friendliness."[7] From both descriptions, one gets a picture of a person not very compelling in physical appearance.

The same can be said of Paul's abilities as a speaker. Paul claims that he lacks the training in rhetoric some of his opponents possess. Given the importance the world of Greece and Rome placed on training in public oratory, some within the Corinthian community looked down upon Paul. "Even if I am untrained in speaking, I am not so in knowledge; in every way we have made this plain to you in all things" (2 Cor 11:6). Indeed, Paul had made this evident to them in a previous letter (see 1 Cor 2:1-5).

Paul views his weaknesses, his lack of personal presence and rhetorical skills, positively. For God's grace to work, Paul's own human personality must retreat to the background. The Corinthian response to Paul's message is based on God's power working through his weakness. Paul's weakness is a significant image since it resembles the weakness and powerlessness of the crucified Christ. What happens in Corinth is a result of God's power working through the lives of individuals. As Acts 9:15 describes, Paul is clearly "a chosen instrument of mine to carry my name before Gentiles, kings, and Israelites."

Paul's Weakness Displayed in Suffering

Paul's description of his sufferings in 2 Corinthians 11:23-33 forms the heart of 2 Corinthians 11:21b–12:10. While Paul refers to his sufferings on behalf of the Gospel on numerous occasions throughout his letters (such as Rom 8:35-36; 1 Cor 4:9-13; 2 Cor 1:3-11; 4:4-11; 6:3-10), this passage is without doubt one of the most vivid displays of human weakness open to God's power.

For Paul, dying with Christ includes identifying with Christ in all the sufferings of daily life. Certainly, as a minister of the Gospel, one's life will more closely imitate the life of the suffering and dying Messiah. The same is true in the life of every follower of Christ. In 2 Corinthians 12:7, Paul speaks of "a thorn in the flesh." This has been variously interpreted as an illness, or perhaps a physical disability, or even a temptation. As an expression, the term "thorn in the flesh" in Hebrew resembles closely the English usage that refers to an adversary that is a persistent irritation and annoyance.[8] Whatever Paul is actually referencing, its significance lies in Paul's purpose in mentioning it. The "thorn in the flesh" is a constant reminder to Paul that his power resides not in himself, but in God. Prior to this verse, Paul had been speaking about some special mystical experiences he had received (12:1-7); a "thorn in the flesh" was given to him "to keep me from being too elated" (12:7). What matters above all is God's power and grace. Everything else remains insignificant.

Insights for Our Own Spiritual Journey: All is Grace

The spiritual significance of Paul's insights here is readily applicable to the spiritual lives of all Christ's followers at every age. All is grace— nothing else is important. We are called to rely upon God's power in all situations. When tempted to boast, Paul shows us that any true boasting relies upon what God's grace has accomplished in our lives, not what we have accomplished by ourselves. Nothing can be achieved without God's grace.

In our culture, we rightly celebrate the achievements of men and women who accomplish much and who contribute much to the good of our society. At the same time, we all rightly strive to succeed by using our gifts, our talents, our education to advance, whether it be at school, college, or in the workplace. However, it is vital that we keep in mind the true Christian perspective for our achievements. Everything we do and achieve takes place within the context of God's grace. All life itself is God's gift. I did not deserve the life I have—it is totally unmerited. Life has been "given" me by God together with the person that I am, with my talents and abilities, and, yes, with my human limitations and weaknesses as well. That is the context in which I live out my life's purpose. As pure gift, pure grace, I respond to this gift of life by using my life's talents and by striving to be the best person I can be. My response to this great gift of life gives true praise and honor to the God who is at the very foundation of my being and without whom I would not exist. True humility acknowledges my relationship with God, my dependence upon God (just as a child depends on the parent, or as a client in the ancient world relied upon his/her patron) for my life and my accomplishments.

God's grace is also the foundation for our spiritual lives. As we have noted above, the Father gave his Son to become human and to die on the cross in order to bring salvation to humanity. This is the greatest gift of all: the gift of God's saving love. The grace of salvation brings us into a relationship with God where we experience God's intense love for us.

The Christian life also embraces and discovers a redemptive meaning in suffering. Experiencing suffering in our present life witnesses to our firm belief in the meaning of the cross and resurrection of Jesus for us. As Pope Benedict XVI testified:

> Christianity is not the easy road; it is, rather, a difficult climb, but one illuminated by the light of Christ and by the great hope that is born of him. Saint Augustine says: Christians are not spared suffering, indeed

they must suffer a little more, because to live the faith expresses the courage to face in greater depth the problems that life and history present. But only in this way, through the experience of suffering, can we know life in its profundity, in its beauty, in the great hope born from Christ crucified and risen again.[9]

Christianity is not a religion of a book, as some tend to say. Rather, it is a religion based upon a person, the person of Christ Jesus. Jesus has shown us that his life culminates in his suffering and death on a cross that was transformed by God's power in raising him from the dead. The Christian life imitates the same pattern. To follow the person of Jesus Christ means "sharing of [Christ's] sufferings by being conformed to his death, if somehow I may attain the resurrection from the dead" (Phil 3:10b-11). The pattern of Jesus' life from suffering through death to the resurrection also offers a valuable lesson for our own spirituality. When one reflects on the suffering and death of Jesus from a purely human point of view, we come to realize how Jesus' life ended in apparent failure: he was rejected by the religious leaders of his own faith and by the political leaders. His own people had welcomed him in such a significant way into the city of Jerusalem, as we recall on Palm Sunday, only to reject and abandon him on Good Friday. What death could be more ignominious than that of Jesus crucified on a cross? In their eyes, Jesus' death ended in failure.

All that changed when the Father raised Jesus from the dead. Jesus' resurrection was a triumph over failure. This triumph was the work of the Father. Here is the secret that Paul discovered at the beginning of his journey in following Christ. At first, Paul too rejected Jesus as a failure: his humiliating death on a cross was proof enough for Paul. But then in his own encounter with the risen Lord, Paul experienced how God the Father reversed this failure into triumph in his resurrection from the dead.

This central truth is significant for our own personal spirituality. We all experience failure at one time or another in our lives so the grace of the crucifixion teaches us there is life beyond failure. God's grace is there to sustain us throughout failures and brings with it the strength and power to overcome whatever comes our way. While our modern culture, especially in our educational systems, drives us always upward and onward to success and accomplishments, nothing in our culture teaches us how to deal with failure. Only our Christian faith offers us the secret to understanding failure. Throughout his life Paul learned the secret that God's grace is always there, sustaining him through his struggles and difficulties. After death, there is always the resurrection. God's grace is there supporting us through failure and ultimately death by bringing us to experience the resurrection.

This is one of the foundational insights Paul's spirituality has bequeathed to us today. Especially in times when we are powerless, when we are weak, the power of God's grace is always there to sustain us though the struggles and failures of our human journey of life. As the Lord says to Paul in the midst of his suffering: "My grace is sufficient for you, for power is made perfect in weakness" (2 Cor 12:9). And Paul concludes his whole reflection in this passage with these words, "for when I am weak, then I am strong" (2 Cor 12:10).

Faith in Christ

"For I am not ashamed of the gospel. It is the power of God for the salvation of everyone who believes: for Jew first, and then Greek. For in it is revealed the righteousness of God from faith to faith; as it is written, 'The one who is righteous by faith will live.'"

(Rom 1:16-17)

Five hundred years ago, the Christian world was embroiled in a bitter and acrimonious debate that stemmed from an interpretation of Paul's spiritual thought. The question, simply put, was: How does a person become just before God? This discussion contributed to the Reformation, where differing answers were given to this question that ultimately caused a split in Western Christianity, a split that has endured to this day. At the heart of the dispute was Paul's assertion, "The one who is righteous by faith will live" (Rom 1:17). This chapter will examine Paul's spiritual understanding of righteousness/justification and how these insights help us to view this issue in a new light.

Peace, Righteousness, and Justification

To understand and appreciate Paul's spirituality better, it is important to explain the basic words and concepts that have caused confusion. In our vocabulary today we often use the phrase, "He is so righteous that he really annoys me!" In this sense, "righteous" is seen negatively and is used almost in the sense of a synonym for "hypocrite." However, in the context of the Scriptures, and particularly in the writings of Paul, the reference to righteousness is understood in a positive light referring to someone who is leading a good and blessed life.

For the people of Israel, peace (*shalom*) is at the heart of all relationships. It refers to good, harmonious relationships between people. Peace is the result of order being established, in the world, in the universe, and in the lives of every one of us. Shalom is that action of God in bringing about order in a divided world, the establishment of right relationships; it brings the world together in harmony. When God is referred to as righteous, the people of Israel as well as Paul are not referring to a quality of God; they are instead speaking about an action of God. The Hebrew people were no abstract thinkers—they were oriented toward action and the same holds true in reference to God as righteous. When God is called righteous, reference is made to God's actions in bringing about peace (*shalom*) and harmony to the world. At the same time that shalom establishes right relationships among people, it implies that relationships within our world have fundamentally broken down. God is the one who can restore these relationships and bring the world together again.

A note needs to be made about the use of the word *righteousness*. Paul's letters are written in Greek, a language that has one root word for this concept of righteousness. However (because of the difficulty in translating Paul's usage of the term), in English two root words are needed to translate this single Greek concept. In English one has a noun *righteousness* and an adjective *righteous,* but no verbal form. One cannot say "to righteous." This means that in English the verbal form of righteous is translated by words such as "*to justify.*" Consequently, in English many different words are used, such as righteous, righteousness, justify, and justification, while in Paul's Greek they are all the same.[1] Whether one speaks of God's righteousness or justification it is exactly the same thing: *God's righteousness is God's justification.*

Relationships Are at the Heart of the Covenant

The Spirituality of the Covenant Is at the Heart of Righteousness

The writer of Genesis 1:1-23 notes that when God created the world, "God saw that it was good." In other words, God's creation conformed to the plan God had for his creation. Peace and harmony existed in the universe since God's order for creation was established and God's plan for the world was initiated. However, that plan was disrupted; peace and harmony in the world were broken through the choices humans made.[2]

The story of the Bible is the story of how God continually reached out to humanity and strove to restore peace and harmony to a disrupted world. God made this plan known through the covenant he established through Abraham. "[The Lord God] took [Abram] outside and said: Look up at the sky and count the stars, if you can. Just so, he added, will your descendants be. Abram put his faith in the Lord, who attributed it to him as an act of righteousness" (Gen 15:5-6). This act of Abraham's faith was regarded by God as an act of righteousness, namely, that he was in a right relationship with God. Through this relationship, Abraham and his descendants would be the ones to extend God's peace to the rest of humanity and the world.

The covenant with Abraham is the context in which the covenant with Israel is to be understood. God's righteousness (God's right actions of salvation for humanity and the world) is demonstrated by choosing a nation, the Israelites, to whom God's revelation came with the intent of bringing peace to the whole world. God establishes a commitment to this nation through a covenant and promised fidelity to this relationship. Israel as a nation, its very identity, is tied up with the covenant God has made with the people, a covenant that was originally initiated with Abraham as the father of the nation and then confirmed through the covenant at Mount Sinai (Exod 19).

The prophets understood well that the covenant with Israel was not intended simply for themselves as a nation, but as a means of restoring peace and harmony to the world by bringing the nations of the world into this relationship with God. The prophet Isaiah paints a beautiful picture of the future age where this peace and harmony is reestablished:

> Then the wolf shall be a guest of the lamb,
>   and the leopard shall lie down with the young goat;
> The calf and the young lion shall browse together,
>   with a little child to guide them. (Isa 11:6)

When one says God is righteous, it means God has remained faithful to this covenantal relationship with the people of Israel. However, Israel did not always remain faithful in carrying out their part in this relationship. God is also righteous in the sense that even when the people of Israel break the covenant, God offers forgiveness and restores them to the relationship.

The Israelites remained true to the covenantal relationship with God by carrying out the law that had come down to them from Moses. While God alone is the one who makes them righteous, a tendency developed among the people of Israel where stress was placed on carrying out faithfully all the stipulations of the law: the focus shifted toward a legalism and their own human effort. By reflecting on these aspects, Paul realized that on one's own it is difficult to remain faithful to these laws; human frailty and human nature made it practically impossible to carry out the stipulations of the law and remain true to this relationship with God. Paul's encounter with the Lord Jesus on the road to Damascus led him to understand that the only path to righteousness was through the power of Christ's grace.

"A New Covenant in My Blood"

Paul's foundational encounter with the risen Lord also led him to reassess his relationship with those traditions that had guided his life until this point. Paul's experience taught him that nothing he had done had earned this new relationship with Christ. God's free exercise of grace was solely responsible. It was a liberating experience Paul termed "freedom in Christ." "For freedom Christ set us free; so stand firm and do not submit again to the yoke of slavery" (Gal 5:1). Paul viewed his life now in Christ very differently from the life he had led before. In his former way of life, Paul believed it was through obedience to the law expressed through "works of the law" that he maintained this covenant relationship with God. Now, in Christ, what is significant is the sole gift of faith with which God has graced Paul. God's grace enabled Paul to remain faithful to the relationship, not his own human efforts or "works of the law."

Paul's experience gave new direction to his spirituality. At the center of his life was his spiritual relationship with Christ in faith. This alone gave meaning and direction to his whole existence, "I long to depart this life and to be with Christ, [for] that is far better" (Phil 1:23). In evaluating his imprisonment in the letter to the Philippians, Paul saw that the outcome of his imprisonment could end either in death or in release. While Paul would have preferred death ("to be with Christ"), he judged that for the sake of the Philippians and Christians elsewhere, the Lord wanted him to continue his work in bringing others into relationship with Christ, "Yet that I remain [in] the flesh is more necessary for your benefit. And this I know with confidence, that I shall remain and continue in the service of all of you for your progress and joy in the faith, so that your boasting in Christ Jesus may abound on account of me when I come to you again" (Phil 1:24-26). This became one of the foundational beliefs Paul expressed throughout his letters. The only path to right relationship with God was through the grace of faith in Christ. Paul's aim in life was to bring others into this same relationship with Christ that he enjoyed. His journey toward the final goal of union with Christ was one he pursued not alone but with all those whom he had brought into relationship with Christ.

Paul's spirituality underwent a transformation through his encounter with the risen Lord. This change occurred not through his own efforts but through the power of God's grace. All was grace. Paul understood his new life in Christ in terms of the covenantal relationship God established. In fact, in speaking of the celebration of the Lord's Supper (the Eucharist) in Corinth, Paul counters abuses that had crept into their celebration by reminding his readers of the words Jesus spoke during the last meal with his disciples when Jesus instructed them to continue to do what he had done:

> For I received from the Lord what I also handed on to you, that the Lord Jesus, on the night he was handed over, took bread, and, after he had given thanks, broke it and said, "This is my body that is for you. Do this in remembrance of me." In the same way also the cup, after supper, saying, "This cup is *the new covenant in my blood.* Do this, as often as you drink it, in remembrance of me." For as often as you eat this bread and drink the cup, you proclaim the death of the Lord until he comes. (1 Cor 11:23-26; italics added)

Paul refers to the *"new covenant in my blood."* God had established a covenant with the people of Israel in the desert and ratified it by means of the blood of animals. This new covenant is established through the shedding of the blood of Jesus on the Cross. It is "new" in the sense that it reestablishes God's covenant through Abraham. As with the covenant with Abraham, this new covenant embraces all peoples, not one exclusive nation. As "apostle to the nations," Paul's task is to bring the peoples of the world into this covenant relationship with Jesus Christ. This new covenant through Jesus Christ brings to fulfillment what was originally intended in the covenant made with Abraham.

As we have seen, the cross and resurrection of Jesus are for Paul the foundational dimensions of his spirituality. A deeper insight into Paul's spirituality emerges from a reflection on the connection he draws between the covenant established by Jesus through his death and the covenant with Abraham:

> Thus Abraham "believed God, and it was credited to him as righteousness."
>
> Realize then it is those who have faith who are children of Abraham. Scripture, which saw in advance that God would justify the Gentiles by faith, foretold the good news to Abraham, saying, "Through you shall all the nations be blessed." Consequently, those who have faith are blessed along with Abraham who had faith. For all who depend on works of the law are under a curse; for it is written, "Cursed be everyone who does not persevere in doing all the things written in the book of the law." And that no one is justified before God by the law is clear, for "the one who is righteous by faith will live." But the law does not depend upon faith; rather, "the one who does these things will live by them." Christ ransomed us from the curse of the law by

becoming a curse for us, for it is written, "Cursed be everyone who hangs on a tree," that the blessings of Abraham might be extended to the Gentiles through Christ Jesus, so that we might receive the promise of the Spirit through faith. (Gal 3:6-14)

This passage is significant. Paul connects the covenant of Jesus with the covenant of Abraham. The covenant Jesus established through his death on the cross made it possible that all who have faith in Christ, whatever their background, are justified. The original intent of the covenant with Abraham is reestablished in Christ. Through faith in God, Abraham was promised descendants from all the nations of the earth. Now in Christ this promise is realized. All who have faith in Christ from the nations of the world are brought into relationship with God and one another. This was something that was never realized through the law.

Later in this same chapter, Paul examines the role the law had played in the past. Its role has led up to the coming of Christ, but now its role has served its function:

Before faith came, we were held in custody under law, confined for the faith that was to be revealed. Consequently, the law was our disciplinarian for Christ, that we might be justified by faith. But now that faith has come, we are no longer under a disciplinarian. For through faith you are all children of God in Christ Jesus. For all of you who were baptized into Christ have clothed yourselves with Christ. There is neither Jew nor Greek, there is neither slave nor free person, there is not male and female; for you are all one in Christ Jesus. And if you belong to Christ, then you are Abraham's descendant, heirs according to the promise. (Gal 3:23-29)

Paul makes a couple of interesting points about the inadequacy of the law in this text. Before faith in Christ came we were "held in custody . . . confined" by the law. Paul is in effect saying the law keeps one in prison.[3] A person is trapped, enslaved by the law and is not able to make a free choice for Christ. The law makes known what should be done, but people are unable to carry out the law because of human weakness. The gift of the Law (the Torah) to Israel was intended to be a guide. Paul compares the law to a "disciplinarian" (Greek, *paidagōgos*). Unfortunately, this translation does not capture the beauty of the comparison Paul is making. The Greek word refers to a slave whose task it was to lead a boy to school and back as well as generally to care for him and ensure his right conduct. Once the boy reached manhood this guide was no longer needed. In this sense, the law operates as a *guide* for the people of Israel on how to lead their lives in relationship with God and one another until the coming of Christ. Once Christ comes, the law is no longer needed. Now that Christ has come, a new stage is opened up in which all the nations of the world are invited into this covenantal relationship with God.

Works of the Torah (Law) and Faith Working in Love

Paul's spirituality shows a dramatic shift in vision. In his former way of life, Paul had adhered to the law and its requirements as faithfully as possible and he saw his actions according to the law as being of utmost value (Phil 3:7). This was a spirituality driven by the law. But now his encounter with Christ has brought him to accept that only through faith in Christ can this relationship with God be maintained. Paul's spirituality is driven by grace.

Paul contrasts these two different spiritual visions starkly in chapter three of his letter to the Philippians. He warned the readers against those who were coming into the community and distorting the message he had preached to them:

> If anyone else thinks he can be confident in flesh, all the more can I. Circumcised on the eighth day, of the race of Israel, of the tribe of Benjamin, a Hebrew of Hebrew parentage, in observance of the law a Pharisee, in zeal I persecuted the church, in righteousness based on the law I was blameless.
>
> [But] whatever gains I had, these I have come to consider a loss because of Christ. More than that, I even consider everything as a loss because of the supreme good of knowing Christ Jesus my Lord. For his sake I have accepted the loss of all things and I consider them so much rubbish, that I may gain Christ and be found in him, not having any righteousness of my own based on the law but that which comes through faith in Christ, the righteousness from God, depending on faith to know him and the power of his resurrection and [the] sharing of his sufferings by being conformed to his death, if somehow I may attain the resurrection from the dead. (Phil 3:4b-11)

Paul contrasts here his present spiritual way of life in Christ to his former life among the people of Israel. Paul's spirituality is once again expressed in terms of the covenant relationship with God. The greatest contrast between these two covenant relationships is found in the fact that his life in Christ comes as a free gift of God. He draws an opposition between the two covenant relationships: the one way of righteousness is attained freely through the grace of Christ, while the other way of righteousness (that he has now rejected), is attained through an identity that began with his birth as a Jew, became established concretely in his circumcision, and finally was maintained through his works of the law. Previously, Paul had placed great importance on his status as a member of the people of Israel and his faithful adherence to the Torah and its implementation: "in righteousness based on the law I was blameless." Now, through his encounter with the risen Lord, he has come to realize that his new covenant relationship with God brings him true freedom. This grace of Christ enabled him to stay true to the relationship; works of the law did not.

Works of the Torah (Law)

> We, who are Jews by nature and not sinners from among the Gentiles, [yet] who know that a person is not justified by works of the law but through faith in Jesus Christ, even we have believed in Christ Jesus that we may be justified by faith in Christ and not by works of the law, because by works of the law no one will be justified. (Gal 2:15-16)

The Torah expressed God's will for God's people and was found in the *written law* that included the Ten Commandments, the Decalogue, and the five Books of Moses (also known as the Pentateuch). The Pharisees had interpreted these laws over time and developed further rules and customs as they adapted the laws of Moses to new contexts and situations. So developed the *oral law* expressing purity rules dealing with daily life that included rituals and food laws. They were identifying markers that showed who was a member of the people of Israel, such as the ritual of circumcision for males. These purity rules were designed to build a wall of separation between the people of Israel and the world outside.

Purity rules offered the people of Israel a structure for their lives to foster right relationships with God and with their fellow Israelites. These purity rules act as part of a socialization process whereby the boundaries are defined between those belonging to the people of Israel and those outside. They are social markers that separate the individual and the community from the wider society. They also define those who have access to God and maintain the right relationships (righteousness) that exist between the individual, the community, and God.[4]

With the advent of the conquests of Alexander the Great (356–323 BC), Hellenistic culture spread throughout the known world. For the people of Israel, it created a significant challenge to their identity and religious way of life. This led to the need to establish boundaries for their own culture and religion. At the time of Paul, Hellenistic culture had become universal throughout the Mediterranean world and exerted enormous pressure for cultural uniformity. As a Pharisee himself, Paul at first saw the need to preserve this wall of distinction between his religion and the polytheistic world around him. Only with his encounter with Christ did Paul come to realize that the risen Lord wanted to embrace all peoples, not build walls of separation among them. A later disciple of Paul expressed this thought well in the letter to the Ephesians:

> But now in Christ Jesus you who once were far off have become near by the blood of Christ.
> For he is our peace, he who made both one and broke down the dividing wall of enmity, through his flesh, abolishing the law with its commandments and legal claims, that he might create in himself one new person in place of the two, thus establishing peace, and might reconcile both with God, in one body, through the cross, putting that enmity to death by it. (Eph 2:13-16)

Paul's new spiritual vision in Christ rejected totally the claim that the people of Israel could maintain a righteous relationship with God through works of the law. As Paul says, "No human being will be justified in his sight by observing the law; for through the law comes consciousness of sin" (Rom 3:20). The law shows one what is sinful, but it cannot enable one to carry out the law. God's grace, given in Christ, on the other hand, does enable one to carry out one's faith through "works of love."

Faith Working through Love

Here, then, is the essential difference between the two alternatives Paul has experienced. One is a covenant righteousness based upon fidelity to the law of Israel, the written and the oral law; the other is a covenant righteousness based upon the relationship with Jesus Christ, a relationship first and foremost initiated by Christ himself through the gift of faith. It is *faith* that makes us righteous (just) and not works of the law as Paul says, "For we consider a person is justified by faith apart from works of the law" (Rom 3:28). Understood in this sense, Martin Luther was undoubtedly right when he spoke of a person being justified by *faith alone.*

Faith means being united to Christ and living his life. The essence of the life of Christ, and one that Christ taught his followers to embrace, was undoubtedly *a life led in love*—love of God and love of one's fellow human being. As Paul says, "For through the Spirit, by faith, we await the hope of righteousness. For in Christ Jesus, neither circumcision nor uncircumcision counts for anything, but only faith working through love" (Gal 5:5-6). Pope Benedict XVI saw that the way in which faith is to be understood is as *faith expressed in love*: "For this reason Luther's phrase: *'faith alone'* is true, if it is not opposed to faith in charity, in love."[5] God's grace initiates this faith and God's grace enables the believer to carry out good deeds in love.

The heart of Paul's spirituality is life with Christ, living a life in relationship with Christ. This means that one leads life as Christ led his, by works of love for others. Pope St. John Paul II expressed this thought of Paul so well when he drew the connection between love and justice:

> Love for others, and in the first place love for the poor, in whom the church sees Christ himself, is made concrete in the promotion of justice. Justice will never be fully attained unless people see in the poor person, who is asking for help in order to survive, not an annoyance or a burden, but an opportunity for showing kindness and a chance for greater enrichment.[6]

Faith is a free gift conferred on the believer. Faith is acquired not through any actions on one's own behalf. This faith is alive. Through the inspiration of the Spirit, faith is expressed in actions that, in essence, are acts of love. Paul expresses these gifts to which the Spirit gives birth in this way:

> In contrast, the fruit of the Spirit is love, joy, peace, patience, kindness, generosity, faithfulness, gentleness, self-control. Against such there is no law. Now those who belong to Christ [Jesus] have crucified their flesh with its passions and desires. If we live in the Spirit, let us also follow the Spirit. (Gal 5:22-25)

Love heads this list. Our identity, shaped by being "in Christ," expresses itself in the love of Christ for others. We will be judged upon our love for others at the Last Judgment as Matthew's Jesus indicates in the parable of the final judgment of the nations (Matt 25:31-46). The central spiritual virtue for Paul is undoubtedly the virtue of love. Paul's spirituality is shaped by the love that has been poured into his heart through the Spirit. "And hope does not disappoint, because the love of God has been poured out into our hearts through the holy Spirit that has been given to us" (Rom 5:5).

Paul develops his spiritual insights into the virtue of love in 1 Corinthians 13 with a hymn that celebrates the significance of love in the life of every believer. Significant aspects of Paul's spirituality emerge from this hymn on the way of living love. The love of the crucified Christ gives shape to everything. This love finds its origin in Christ's love for humanity. It is a love that frees every believer to live for others just as Christ led his life for others. "I have been crucified with Christ; yet I live, no longer I, but Christ lives in me; insofar as I now live in the flesh, I live by faith in the Son of God who has loved me and given himself up for me" (Gal 2:19b-20).

In 1 Corinthians 13 Paul lists seven positive qualities of love and eight negative aspects:

> Love is patient, love is kind. It is not jealous, [love] is not pompous, it is not inflated, it is not rude, it does not seek its own interests, it is not quick-tempered, it does not brood over injury, it does not rejoice over wrongdoing but rejoices with the truth. It bears all things, believes all things, hopes all things, endures all things.
> Love never fails. (1 Cor 13:4-8)

At the heart of this list of love's qualities is the statement that love "does not seek its own interests." The Greek phrase, *ou zētei ta heautēs*, refers to desiring something for oneself alone. Previously in 1 Corinthians 10:33 Paul said, "I try to please everyone in every way, not seeking my own benefit but that of the many, that they may be saved." This passage makes clear what Paul's spiritual vision is: he looks to what is best for others (not for himself) so he can bring them to salvation. For Paul, the essence of love, seen from a negative viewpoint, embraces "not seeking one's own advantage." Positively, it seeks the advantage of others. It is not self-centered, but other centered.

In the context of Paul's other letters, his statement that love "does not seek its own interests" bears a special spiritual significance. Philippians 2 contains another beautiful hymn where Paul reflects on Christ Jesus' path through humiliation to exaltation. In the context of introducing this hymn to his readers, Paul speaks about love and instructs the Philippians in this way:

> If there is any encouragement in Christ, *any solace in love,* any participation in the Spirit, any compassion and mercy, complete my joy by being of the same mind, *with the same love,* united in heart, thinking one thing . . . Each looking out not for his own interests, but [also] everyone for those of others.

Have among yourselves the same attitude that is also yours in
Christ Jesus,

Who, though he was in the form of God. . . . (Phil 2:1-2, 4-6; italics added)

This hymn defines Paul's spirituality very clearly. Again the context of
love shapes everything, especially how one relates to another. Paul calls
on his readers to have the same attitude whereby one looks first to the interests of others rather than to one's own interest. This spiritual approach
emulates the same attitude of Christ Jesus. He gave up his status with
God and emptied himself by becoming human and by further humbling
himself to death on the cross. This is the story of Christ Jesus' love for
humanity, presented as the example that followers of Christ should embrace: he was humiliated to the point of death on the cross for the sake of
humanity. This love of Christ Jesus is what Michael Gorman calls "Cruciform love"—this is the love we are called to emulate in our own lives:

> Cruciform love is faith in action. It does not seek its own good but
> the good of others. Indeed, for the good of others it renounces the
> use of certain rights. Cruciform love edifies others and never harms
> them, not even enemies. It never retaliates or uses violence. . . .
> Cruciform love, in a word, continues the story of the cross in new
> times and places. Cruciform love is imaginative.[7]

Insights for Our Own Spiritual Journey: Faith Expressed in Acts of Love

Spirituality Open to Change

Paul's spirituality shows remarkable growth and transformation. He
was dedicated to his Hebrew faith and strengthened by his study of the
Hebrew Scriptures. God's grace changed all that completely through
Paul's encounter with the risen Christ. God's transforming grace led
his journey down another path, one he had previously rejected so force-
fully. God's spiritual transformation of Paul set in motion the divine
plan for the salvation of all the nations of the world. Paul is a testimony
to every one of us that we must never let our spiritual lives stagnate or
become so firmly entrenched that we are unable, through God's grace,
to grow and change. God's grace works in surprising ways, as Paul's
life certainly testifies. Openness to God's actions in our lives allows
God to take control—with God's grace surprising things happen.

Spirituality Directed by the Firm Belief that All Is Grace

Faith as a gift comes undeservedly from God. Nothing we do earns this gift. Faith is totally gratuitous, given us through the grace that comes from Jesus' death on the cross and creating a new identity for us in Christ. For the people of Israel, their identity came from the status they inherited by birth as members of the nation of Israel. As we have seen, Paul rejected this because the focus lay on himself rather than on God. Performing works of the law were seen as proof of being in this covenant relationship with God. In the ultimate analysis, Paul stressed that our covenant relationship with God comes through Christ, not through our status or by our own actions. I do nothing to earn that relationship since it all comes through the free gift of Christ.

The arguments of the sixteenth century that led to the Protestant Reformation were concerned with this concept of justification/righteousness that Martin Luther viewed as Paul's central teaching: namely, that one's identity as a Christian is not a result of personal merit—it comes through the outpouring of God's Spirit that communicates the effects of Christ's salvation, his death on the Cross. When the disputes between Roman Catholics and Reformers took place, each side tended to overstate its positions as well as that of its opponents. For example, Martin Luther considered that Roman Catholics were emphasizing the ability to earn salvation themselves through good deeds they performed. In October 1999, Roman Catholics and most Lutheran churches reached an agreement in which each side clarified its own positions and showed that it did in fact share a common understanding of justification/righteousness, that God's free gift of salvation was accomplished by Jesus Christ once and for all through his death on the cross:

> In faith we together hold the conviction that justification is the work of the triune God. The Father sent his Son into the world to save sinners. The foundation and presupposition of justification is the incarnation, death, and resurrection of Christ. Justification thus means that Christ himself is our righteousness, in which we share through the Holy Spirit in accord with the will of the Father. Together we confess: By grace alone, in faith in Christ's saving work and not because of any merit on our part, we are accepted by God and receive the Holy Spirit, who renews our hearts while equipping and calling us to good works.[8]

Paul's spirituality teaches us that our identity is shaped by being in Christ. Our faith comes to us through God's gift of grace. In baptism we are brought into relationship with God in Christ, and this relationship is sustained and enriched through acts of love. Since our identity is shaped through Christ's death on the cross, our spirituality is indeed a "cruciform spirituality" where we place the other first, before ourselves. These are the foundational elements for Paul's spirituality and are also foundational elements that Roman Catholics and Lutherans today share. What is remarkable in our present Christian world is that, through openness to God's Spirit and reflection in that same Spirit on Paul's spirituality anew, what divided Christians in the past is now seen as something that unites them. At last that wall of separation, "the wall of justification by faith alone," erected some five hundred years ago between Catholics and Lutherans, has now been broken down. God's grace accomplishes surprising things.

Spirituality Illustrated through Acts of Love

God's gift of faith needs to be expressed in acts of love. From Paul's perspective, works of the law do not lead to faith, but faith in its turn flowers forth into works of love. Sometimes the letter of James is depicted as contradicting Paul's thought. For example, in James 2:14-16, the writer develops his argument that faith without works is dead. From the previous examination of Paul's spirituality and his understanding of God's righteousness, it is clear that Paul and James are not in opposition to each other. Each one's focus lies with different aspects of the relationship between faith and actions. For Paul, the stress lies on how we come to faith. Faith is God's free gift to us. Our identity comes from God's gift of grace. James, on the other hand, wishes to stress that while we already have faith it is necessary for a person to express that faith in action. Paul is concerned largely with the period before coming to faith, while James is concerned about the after-effects of faith. Both Paul and James agree and show that faith is active in love. Together Paul and James complement each other and together they offer the fullest insight into the understanding of the relationship between faith and action.

Paul's spirituality distances itself from two tendencies that sometimes appear in popular spiritual traditions. The one tendency is to focus too much on what one does. There is nothing a person does that earns his or her salvation. Sometimes there is the thought that if a person says certain prayers God will reward him, if a person performs certain actions, God will protect her. Do not misunderstand me: praying to God and asking for God's protection are truly admirable, but we are not making a contract with God: humans do X so God will give them Y. All actions, prayers, lives are inspired by love. It is the same as in any human relationship: a true relationship is centered upon love. When someone does things for another person, one does them out of love, not for what one can gain from these actions.

Paul's spirituality demonstrates so well what is true of every relationship. God's love has invited us into the covenant relationship that his Son established through his death on the cross; the gift of faith inspires us to respond with acts of love. These works of love are directed toward our neighbor.

A second tendency or misunderstanding arises when the focus is placed solely on the relationship between God and oneself. One tends to forget that God's transforming love should lead us to express love for God in personal actions toward our neighbors. In celebrating "the Lord's supper," "the new covenant," "in remembrance of . . . the death of the Lord until he comes" (1 Cor 11:20-26), we experience once again the presence of God's Son and the gift of his Body and his Blood for us; we are called to go out and care for the most needy members of the Body of Christ, the church. The transforming grace of God's love, God's righteousness, inspires us to respond through acts of love for the poor. As one of the dismissals at the end of Mass urges us, "Go in peace, glorifying the Lord by your life!"

Christian Spirituality does not start with laws and rules, but is founded upon and sustained by a relationship with Christ, both personal and communal. The grace of Christ establishes our relationship with God that expresses itself in love for one's neighbor. Nothing "will be able to separate us from the love of God in Christ Jesus our Lord" (Rom 8:39).

Humanity Renewed in Christ

"For just as in Adam all die, so too in Christ shall all be brought to life"

(1 Cor 15:22)

Fallen Humanity's Sin through Adam

To appreciate more fully this new redeemed person in Christ, we examine two aspects of Paul's understanding: fallen humanity through Adam and how humanity becomes a new creation through Christ. Our faith tells us there is only one God, a God who is good, a God who created the world as good (Gen 1:10). God's creation corresponded to God's plan. However, God also created human beings with the gift of freedom and free choice, "You are free to eat from any of the trees of the garden except the tree of knowledge of good and evil" (Gen 2:16-17). God did not intend to force humanity's acceptance. God gave the human being free will to choose whether to remain in relationship with God or to reject God. The human person was free to make the choice of doing what God commanded, or rejecting it. By choosing to go against the will of God, humanity rejected the good. This is where evil enters in. Evil does not come from a source that exists as though it were some entity in competition with God. Evil comes from the freedom humanity has, a freedom that is abused. We could say evil is the absence of good. It is like a T-shirt with a hole in it: just as the hole is the absence of the material of the T-shirt that should be there, evil is the absence of the good that should be there.

In the letter to the Romans, Paul presents an outline of his teaching on the nature and origin of sin (5:12-21). His purpose is to place in greater relief the grace of Christ and what he accomplished for us through his death on the cross. We cannot appreciate the significance of Christ's gift of grace unless we are aware of the situation of humanity before Christ came. In this passage from the letter to the Romans, Paul contrasts Adam with the person of Christ. Paul's main concern is not with Adam and the consequences of his sin for humanity, but rather on

Christ and the grace that has transformed humanity through his death and resurrection:

> Therefore, just as through one person sin entered the world, and through sin, death, and thus death came to all, inasmuch as all sinned—for up to the time of the law, sin was in the world, though sin is not accounted when there is no law. But death reigned from Adam to Moses, even over those who did not sin after the pattern of the trespass of Adam, who is the type of the one who was to come. (Rom 5:12-14)

Behind this passage lies the Genesis story where Adam and Eve use their God-given freedom to reject God and their relationship with God (Gen 3:1-24). In this story, the biblical author is reflecting, under God's inspiration, on the condition of frail humanity. Through a story about our first parents, we are offered some significant insights into our human condition that have importance for every age. In the first instance, the writer gives an understanding of sin and its consequences. The sin of Adam reveals the true nature of sin as an act of disobedience to God by which the human person rejects God's command and is placed in opposition to God. Added to this, the writer shows that at the heart of every act of disobedience to God lies an internal reflection and decision. As in the story of Adam and Eve, sinners make themselves the measure of all things and replace God by deciding for themselves what is good or evil. They refuse to accept their dependence upon God, destroying their relationship with God and with one another. The consequences of this sin led first of all to the rupture of relationships: their unity with God was broken and their interaction with each other was harmed. The human person alone caused this rupture in relationships.

This estrangement continued on to the next generation as is demonstrated by the story of Cain's murder of his brother, Abel (Gen 4:18). The story of the Bible is an ongoing commentary on these broken relationships between humans and God, and between humans themselves. All these accounts illustrate the fragmentation of human nature. Every human being is born into a situation of alienation from God, from one another, and from him/herself.

A further consequence of the sin of Adam was that death entered our world through the first parents' rejection of God. Death always embodies the consequences of this rejection and remains a reminder to the human race that all have sinned. The book of Wisdom illustrates this belief well:

> For God formed us to be imperishable;
>> the image of his own nature he made us.
> But by the envy of the devil, death entered the world;
>> and they who are allied with him experience it.
>>> (Wis 2:23-24)

What is remarkable in the Adam and Eve story is, despite the dire consequences that result from their actions, God still offers hope for a future where evil will be conquered:

> I will put enmity between you and the woman,
>> and between your offspring and hers;
> They will strike at your head,
>> while you strike at their heel. (Gen 3:15)

Christian tradition has understood this passage as the first promise of a redeemer where the snake is interpreted as referring to the devil, and the offspring of the woman is taken as a reference to the person of Christ whose task is to destroy the works of the devil.

The evil committed by Adam has had enormous consequences for the whole human race. Each one of us is born into the human family where we experience in our own lives this fragmentation or alienation with God, ourselves, and one another. Our own sins confirm this reality—no one is without sin. This situation into which we as humans have been born has been termed "the state of original sin." This term was not used by Paul, neither is it a term found in the Scriptures. However, it is a term that has developed within Christian tradition as Christians have reflected on this biblical narrative through the lens of human experience. "Original sin" refers to this ancestral sin of Adam and Eve and the consequences that have arisen as a result of this first sin. Romans 5:12-14, as referred to above, is the classic text that forms the foundation for this teaching on original sin: "Therefore, just as through one person sin entered the world, and through sin, death, and thus death came to all, inasmuch as all sinned. . . ." Adam's sin has hurt the human race in two specific ways: *Death* came into the world as a consequence of Adam's rejection of God. And human beings are born now into *a situation of sin*, a situation of alienation from God. As Paul says in Romans 5:19, "For just as through the disobedience of one person the many were many sinners, so through obedience of one the many will be made righteous."

The Catholic writer G. K. Chesterton said the doctrine of original sin is the one doctrine that is so easily demonstrable.[1] Today we see as well how our actions affect one another. For example, with regard to the environment, we have become more and more conscious of how our actions in burning carbon fuels and how our consumer-infected society and "throw-away" culture are eroding the world we inhabit together. One cannot say one's evil actions only affect oneself. Such actions undoubtedly have an effect on others and, like a virus, that effect spreads. Such was the sin of Adam: it had the enormous consequence that it ultimately brought death into the world, and with it alienation from God, one another, and oneself.

However, there is the other side of the coin as well. The actions of one person can also affect the lives of so many for good. Think of the life of Blessed Mother Teresa of Calcutta. Her acts of concern for the poorest of the poor have inspired many people today to embrace a concern for the less fortunate in society. Mother Teresa's inspiration for compassion came from Christ himself. His death and resurrection on our behalf makes it possible for us and billions of other humans to become new creatures through the grace of faith he has bestowed.

A New Creation in Christ

In Romans 5:15-21 Paul goes on to show that Christ's resurrection changed forever humanity's situation that began with Adam's rejection of God. Reflecting on the death and resurrection of Christ, Paul shows how Christ reversed what happened through Adam. As Paul says in 1 Corinthians, "So it is written, 'The first man, Adam, became a living being,' the last Adam a life-giving spirit" (15:45). Paul is clear: he makes a strong contrast between Adam and Christ (whom he refers to as "the last Adam"). Just as Adam marked the beginning of the first creation, Christ is the beginning of a new creation. Adam's rejection of his relationship with God brought about alienation from God, from one another, and from oneself. In the new creation, Christ began a reversal whereby humans are restored in Christ to their relationship with God, one another, and themselves.

In Romans 5:12-14 Paul traced the history of salvation from Adam, through the law, and ultimately to Christ. Now in 5:15-21 Paul places the focus on Jesus Christ and the all-important grace he has showered upon humanity. Paul stresses this strongly when he says "For if by that one person's transgression the many died, how much more did the grace of God and the gracious gift of the one person Jesus Christ overflow for the many" (Rom 5:15). In making the contrast between Adam and the person of Christ, Paul stresses how much more Christ's actions have transcended Adam's sin. Ultimately, Paul comes to show how the gift (or the grace) Christ has given us through his death and resurrection far outweighs everything that happened through the sin of Adam, "Where sin increased, grace overflowed all the more" (Rom 5:20). This is the most consoling aspect of the human condition: the power of God's grace far outweighs the sin experienced in our world.

The grace of the risen Christ transforms those who embrace Christ and makes them into a new creation where their relationships are now restored to what God intended at the beginning of creation. Human beings were unable to accomplish this for themselves—it comes undeservedly through the grace of the risen Christ. The consequences of death are also reversed. Just as Christ has risen from the dead, so believers as a new creation in Christ also share in the resurrection. Their transformation begins now, but they will experience its fullness in the life to come.

Insights for Our Own Spiritual Journey

The importance of Paul's insights into the human condition is foundational for our spirituality. Paul captures the human condition so well when he addresses the struggle we all experience in life in the image of a civil war he sees going on within himself:

> What I do, I do not understand. For I do not do what I want, but I do what I hate . . . For I know that good does not dwell in me, that is, in my flesh. The willing is ready at hand, but doing the good is not. For I do not do the good I want, but I do the evil I do not want. . . . Who will deliver me from this mortal body? Thanks be to God through Jesus Christ our Lord. (Rom 7:15, 18-19, 24-25)

Here Paul gives expression to the inner struggle at the center of our being. We experience the tension of being pulled in two directions. The only way to overcome this conflict is through the grace and power of Christ. Paul is in effect saying, "I know what is good, but I do not have the power to withstand the pull that comes from my human nature to reject the good. Only the power of Christ's grace makes it possible for me to do the good." This is a concrete illustration of how our human nature has been infected by the sin of Adam—we are weakened, but the grace of Christ is far more powerful.

"Thanks be to God through Jesus Christ our Lord" (Rom 7:25): Every Christian can echo these words of Paul. We can echo them because of our

own experience of how the grace of Christ works in our lives, enabling us to overcome the struggles of our own human existence. Our spirituality teaches us that alone we can accomplish nothing. Only through the grace of Christ are we able to overcome our evil impulses. The gift of the cross and resurrection has given every believer not only hope but also strength to carry out the way of life that Jesus Christ mapped out for us. Our faith assures us that the human condition into which we are born can and is overcome by the grace of Christ working within the lives of each believer. Perhaps we could put it this way: the virus of sin that has infected human nature from the beginning has found in Christ Jesus' death and resurrection its antidote. The grace of Christ that comes from the gift of Christ's cross and resurrection works in our lives to overcome the virus of sin and the evil tendencies that are a consequence of sin. We are healed through the grace of Christ. Just as humans rely on an antidote to destroy a virus, so Christians rely upon the power of the cross, the power of God's grace, to "*neutralize* its poison"[2] and restore each person to act as the creation God intended in the very beginning.

A Spirituality of Transformation: As Christians we believe the grace of the death and resurrection of Christ truly transforms us into a new creation. Through baptism and the sacraments we are no longer the same. We are restored through Christ into a new relationship with God, with one another, and with ourselves. God's Spirit communicates the grace of Christ to us, transforming us into children of God. We are not simply named God's children; we truly become God's children. A real transformation occurs within the center of our being where God comes to dwell within each one of us. Transformed by the grace of Christ, the very life of God is communicated to us and we are brought into a deep, committed relationship with God. This grace empowers one to lead a life to do good and avoid evil. The same transformation happens to every believer, every follower of Christ, everyone who has received the grace of Christ through the power of the Spirit in baptism. As such, we are all in the same relationship with God, one another, and with ourselves. We have all become God's children and entered into the new covenant that Christ has ratified through his blood on the cross. This has very real consequences. As children of God, we are all equal in dignity, and there should be no form of distinctions or discrimination of anyone. Through the grace of Christ we are empowered to live and celebrate our lives as new creations in Christ.

The grace of Christ has healed the wounded human person. As humans, we are not living in a pessimistic state without hope, where we are doomed to perpetuate a life of false choices. Instead, the power of Christ's grace overcomes our weakness and inabilities by empowering us to choose what is good. That is why we can shout out with Paul, "Thanks be to God through Christ Jesus our Lord" (Rom 7:25).

Community-Oriented Spirituality

"I urge you therefore, brothers, by the mercies of God, to offer your bodies as a living sacrifice, holy and pleasing to God, your spiritual worship."

(Rom 12:1)

Without doubt the question "How do we connect to the 'Yes' of Jesus to the Father?" is foundational for our spirituality and central to Paul's spiritual vision. As members of the human race, we are all connected to Adam through our biological nature. His "No" to God infected all human history and all who are born into the human family. We have seen how our human nature had been fragmented and our relationships at every level had been broken. We are all heirs to the original sin of the first Adam. This insight gives rise to the all-important question, "How does one become part of this new beginning that Jesus has won for humanity?" Paul's answer to this question is clear and simple: "Through the Holy Spirit." When people are born into this world, their biological nature connects them with the human race and its alienation from God and other human beings. Now their rebirth as a new creation occurs through the power of the Holy Spirit. This chapter examines the role the Holy Spirit plays in making me a new creation in Christ as well as the effects and consequences the gift of the Spirit has for one's spiritually as an individual as well as part of the community of the Body of Christ.

Experiencing the Gift of the Spirit as Foundational for Paul's Spirituality

We attribute to Paul the use of the term "Holy Spirit" (1 Cor 6:19), and it is from Paul that Christian theology has largely derived its teachings on the Spirit. Paul's understanding of the Spirit, rooted in his heritage within the people of Israel, developed and grew through his own experience of the Spirit working in his life and in the communities he founded. For Paul, the Spirit was the way the newness of the Christ event was communicated to those who believed in Christ Jesus.

The Spirit in the Old Testament

In Hebrew the word for Spirit is *ruah* (in Greek, *pneuma*). At its core, *ruah* refers to the movement of air that embraces the wind as well as the breath of human life. For the people of Israel, the most powerful force of nature they experienced was the power of the wind. They used this concept of the wind to capture the idea of God's almighty creating power, as can be seen at the beginning of the creation story where the biblical writer gives the following description, "In the beginning, when God created the heavens and the earth—and the earth was without form or shape, with darkness over the abyss and *a mighty wind sweeping* over the waters" (Gen 1:1-2; italics added). In the second creation story, when God creates the human person, the writer gives the following description, "Then the LORD God formed the man out of the dust of the ground and *blew into his nostrils the breath of life,* and the man became a living being" (Gen 2:7; italics added). God breathes into this human person the breath of life and Adam becomes a living being. When a person dies, the breath of life escapes. This very life element of the human person comes from God, from God's breath or God's Spirit, and departs from the human person at death.

The Spirit of God in the Old Testament also refers to that gift or force that empowers human beings to accomplish some special activity. For example, Samson's great strength is attributed to God's Spirit, "But the spirit of the LORD rushed upon Samson, and he tore the lion apart barehanded, as one tears a young goat" (Judg 14:6). The prophets as well were gifted with God's Spirit when they spoke in God's name:

> The spirit of the LORD God is upon me,
>   because the LORD has anointed me;
> He has sent me to bring good news to the afflicted,
>   to bind up the brokenhearted . . . (Isa 61:1)

After exile, the people of Israel no longer experienced God's Spirit working among them; nevertheless, they had the expectation that in the final times God's Spirit would again raise the people of Israel back to life. The prophet Ezekiel paints the memorable vision where bones of the dead are raised to life through the power of the Spirit. The Lord interprets this vision for Ezekiel in this way, "Look! I am going to open your graves; I will make you come up out of your graves, my people, and bring you back to the land of Israel. . . . I will put my spirit in you that you may come to life, and I will settle you in your land" (Ezek 37:12, 14). Paul was to view the resurrection of Jesus as a beginning of the fulfillment of this prophecy.

Paul's Understanding of the Spirit

For Paul, the role of the Spirit is foundational for spirituality since the Spirit is at the core of our identity as followers of Christ. At Pentecost, the Spirit came down upon the apostles gathered together, "Then there appeared to them tongues as of fire, which parted and came to rest on each one of them. And they were all filled with the holy Spirit and began to speak in different tongues, as the Spirit enabled them to proclaim" (Acts 2:3-4). The account goes on to describe how people from all parts of the known world listened to the apostles address them "speaking in their own tongues" (Acts 2:11). This whole episode (Acts 2:1-13) stresses how a new humanity is created out of the diverse peoples of the world through the power of God's Spirit. What happened at the beginning of humanity in the story of the Tower of Babel (Gen 11:1-9) is now reversed through the death and resurrection of Christ. This account shows that God's intent is to bring humanity together again within a community where the differences among people are of no value and the common language of faith in Jesus Christ unites everyone in worship of the same God. The workings of the Holy Spirit occur within the context of a community of believers as well as in the lives of individuals whom the Spirit draws into this community.

Paul always understood the Spirit in a dynamic way, as its core meaning implies. Spirit implies an action rather than a static entity. Paul's own experience of God's Spirit working in his life and in the life of the Christian communities brought him to a deeper awareness of the meaning of the Spirit than he had previously. Now, for Paul, God's Spirit is a real person responsible for the new life the believer now leads.

God's Spirit

When Paul refers to the Spirit of God, he understands above all God's activity in relation to the world and to humanity. Paul never speculates about the essence or the ontology of God. Instead, God's Spirit refers to God's action of power. God's power is seen not only in the context of miraculous actions that God performs but also, as noted previously, in the way that God's power works in transforming human weakness, "For when I am weak, then I am strong" (2 Cor 12:10). The Spirit is also spoken about in personal terms, as seen in the Spirit's role of leading us to pray in the right manner:

> In the same way, the Spirit too comes to the aid of our weakness; for we do not know how to pray as we ought, but the Spirit itself intercedes with inexpressible groanings. And the one who searches hearts knows what is the intention of the Spirit, because it intercedes for the holy ones according to God's will. (Rom 8:26-27)

The Spirit and the Flesh

Paul also speaks about the human spirit as the people of Israel were accustomed to do. The human spirit is not the same as the Greek concept of the soul (as opposed to the body). For the people of Israel, the human spirit is the innermost self, the center of one's being, as Paul says, "Among human beings, who knows what pertains to a person except the spirit of the person that is within? Similarly, no one knows what pertains to God except the Spirit of God" (1 Cor 2:11).

The human spirit is that place where God and the human person interact on the most foundational level. Here God's Spirit connects with the human spirit and transforms it. The transforming power of God's Spirit overcomes human weakness and enables the human person to accomplish things it was previously unable to do:

> I say, then: live by the Spirit and you will certainly not gratify the desire of the flesh. For the flesh has desires against the Spirt, and the Spirit against the flesh; these are opposed to each other, so that you may not do what you want. But if you are guided by the Spirit, you are not under the law. (Gal 5:16-18)

Paul contrasts here the desires of the Spirit and the desires of the flesh. Paul is referring first of all to the power God's Spirit has infused into the human spirit. God's Spirit, simply put, is at work in the lives of believers. Previously, in his letter to the Galatians, Paul had spoken about God's transforming power working in the lives of believers, "Does, then, the one who supplies the Spirit to you and works mighty deeds among you do so from works of the law or from faith in what you heard?" (Gal 3:5). The obstacle to the working of God's Spirit is the flesh. By "the flesh" Paul does not intend the human body, but rather whatever is opposed to or hinders God's effective working within the lives of believers, such as the vices Paul goes on to list in Galatians 5:19-21: "Now the works of the flesh are obvious: immorality, impurity, licentiousness, idolatry, sorcery, hatreds, rivalry, jealousy, outbursts of fury, acts of selfishness, dissensions, factions, occasions of envy, drinking bouts, orgies, and the like. I warn you, as I warned you before, that those who do such things will not inherit the kingdom of God." The flesh refers to those tendencies, desires, or vices that pull one away from God working within our lives. Paul is not distinguishing between "the soul and the body" but rather contrasting God's power (the Spirit) working in our lives and with those aspects that resist God's working (the flesh):

> Hence, now there is no condemnation for those who are in Christ Jesus. For the law of the [S]pirit of life in Christ Jesus has freed you from the law of sin and death. For what the law, wakened by the flesh, was powerless to do, this God had done: by sending his own Son in the likeness of sinful flesh and for the sake of sin, he condemned sin in the flesh, so that the righteous decree of the law might be fulfilled in us, who live not according to the flesh but according to the [S]pirit. (Rom 8:1-4)[1]

In these verses, Paul indicates beautifully how God's Spirit transforms the lives of believers in such a dramatic fashion that they are able to accomplish what on their own they were never able to do. The power of the Spirit working with the human spirit enables the believer to overcome the power of the flesh. The Spirit draws the human person toward God rather than away from God.

In the rest of Romans 8, Paul reflects on how this gift of the Spirit transforms the lives of Christians. The Spirit comes to dwell within the believer, communicating the life of the risen Christ to the believer: "If the Spirit of the one who raised Jesus from the dead dwells in you, the one who raised Christ from the dead will give life to your mortal bodies also, through his Spirit that dwells in you" (Rom 8:11). Christians are promised that not only will this same Spirit empower them to overcome the hostile forces of the flesh here in this earthly journey but also that they will inherit the kingdom of God. The transforming power of the Spirit will also communicate to Christians what Jesus himself has received, the resurrection from the dead. The consequences of Adam's sin in us are reversed. While death was the result of Adam's sin, now the promise of the resurrection of the dead is a consequence of Jesus' death.

The Christians' transformed life is a real transformation: "For those who are led by the Spirit of God are children of God. For you did not receive a spirit of slavery to fall back into fear, but you received a spirit of adoption, through which we cry, 'Abba, Father'" (Rom 8:14-15). Through the Spirit, Christians become members of the family of God. As Jesus

Christ is the Son of God, so through the power of God's Spirit Christians become Jesus' brothers and sisters who worship God as Abba (Father).

How Does the Holy Spirit Become My Spirit?

The question remains, "How does one *personally* become a part of this community of the family of God? How does one experience the transforming power of the Spirit in his or her own life?" Paul provides an answer to these questions in a number of ways. The connection happens through the power of the Spirit in a twofold way: through the proclamation of the word and through the sacraments.

The Proclamation of the Word

The power of the Spirit works mysteriously within the heart drawing a person toward union with God. Paul tells us specifically how this happens in Romans 10 where he begins with a quotation from the Book of Deuteronomy (30:14), "But what does it say? 'The word is near you, / in your mouth and in our heart' / (that is, the word of faith that we preach), for if you confess with your mouth that Jesus is Lord and believe in your heart that God raised him from the dead, you will be saved" (Rom 10:8-9). Paul shows that it all begins with the proclamation of the word of God that he (and other apostles) preach, a proclamation that continues down to this day, especially when the sacraments are celebrated within the community. Faith comes from listening to the word of God being proclaimed, as Paul describes:

> But how can they call on him in whom they have not believed? And how can they believe in him of whom they have not heard? And how can they hear without someone to preach? And how can people preach unless they are sent? . . . Thus faith comes from what is heard, and what is heard comes through the word of Christ. (Rom 10:14-15, 17)

When the word of God is proclaimed, the Holy Spirit touches the hearts of listeners to be receptive to the message. This happens within the center of the person's being, with the Holy Spirit drawing the person into a relationship with God and bringing him or her into communion with God and with others who have experienced similar encounters. As Pope Benedict says, "Faith does not come from reading but from listening. It is not only something interior but also a relationship with Someone. It implies an encounter with the proclamation; it implies the existence of the Other, whom it proclaims, and creates communion."[2]

The Sacraments

Paul does not use the word *sacrament*. This term developed within the early Christian tradition as Christians reflected on the message of Paul and the rest of the New Testament within the context of their own experiences in celebrating the liturgy.

Baptism: The proclamation of the word is realized through the sacrament of baptism. The one who hears the word enters into relationship with the risen Lord through the sacrament of baptism. Paul describes this connection between baptism and the death and resurrection of Jesus so eloquently when he writes, "Or are you unaware that we who were baptized into Christ Jesus were baptized into his death? We were indeed buried with him through baptism into death, so that, just as Christ was raised from the dead by the glory of the Father, we too might live in newness of life" (Rom 6:3-4). Paul derived this imagery from the way Christians were being baptized at that time. As Jesus was taken down from the cross and placed in a tomb from which he was raised three days later, so the one being baptized would go down into the water of a baptismal pool and then rise from it. In baptism, the believer symbolically goes down into the tomb and is buried with Christ. One dies to one's former way of life and then, through the sacrament, rises from the waters of baptism a totally new creation. The death and resurrection of Christ become reality in the life of the one baptized. Baptism constitutes a new beginning, a new life that is led through the power of the Holy Spirit.

The sacrament of baptism brings the believer into union with Christ and with the community. For Paul, the phrase "in Christ" gives expression to this union with Christ and the community. Paul speaks of a number of variations on this phrase: "through Christ," "into Christ," "with Christ," and "belonging to Christ."[3] These phrases capture the way of uniting individual Christians and the community with the death and resurrection of Jesus Christ. He became one of us, shared in our human nature (including our suffering and death), and was transformed by the resurrection (Phil 2:5-11). Because Jesus shared in our humanity and died on our behalf, we can now share in his glorified humanity in this life and have the hope of the future resurrected life. "I have been crucified with Christ; yet, I live, no longer I, but Christ lives in me" (Gal 2:19-20) and "we were indeed buried with him through baptism into death" (Rom 6:4). In this way Paul expresses what salvation in Christ really means: a foundational transformation in the life of the Christian and the community. In this way we live "in Christ" and "Christ lives in me and you." "Thus 'Christ in me/you' is a kind of shorthand for '(the Spirit of) Christ dwelling in you,' referring to the spiritual presence of the risen Christ that empowers and directs the community from within."[4] The whole process of coming into union with Christ and the Christian community is under the guidance and inspiration of the Holy Spirit. Through the power of the Holy Spirit, the spiritual life that comes from the cross and resurrection of Christ continues to influence the lives of all faithful Christians.

The Eucharist: The Spirit of God also communicates the effects of Christ's death and resurrection to the Christian through the sacrament of the Eucharist.[5] Paul offers the earliest account of the institution of the Eucharist in the entire New Testament, preceding the account in the Gospel of Mark, the first gospel to be written, by some fifteen years:

> For I received from the Lord what I also handed on to you, that the Lord Jesus, on the night he was handed over, took bread, and, after he had given thanks, broke it and said, "This is my body that is for you. Do this in remembrance of me." In this same way also the cup, after supper, saying, "This cup is the new covenant in my blood. Do this, as often as you drink it, in remembrance of me." For as often as you eat this bread and drink the cup, you proclaim the death of the Lord until he comes. (1 Cor 11:23-26)

In this tradition of the institution of the Eucharist, Jesus identifies his action with the covenants of the Old Testament. As the previous covenants had been established through the shedding of blood, the same is true of this new covenant, but now it is inaugurated through Jesus' own blood shed on the cross. Jesus' words of institution make a direct connection to the covenant God established with the people of Israel at Mount Sinai, "Then [Moses] took the blood and splashed it on the people, saying, 'This is the blood of the covenant which the LORD has made with you according to all these words'" (Exod 24:8). Jesus' words also make a connection with the promises of the prophets, especially the prophet Jeremiah, when Jesus identifies the cup as "the new covenant in my blood." Jeremiah had looked toward the future where he saw that God would establish a "new covenant" with his people: "See the days are coming—oracle of the LORD—when I will make a new covenant with the house of Israel and the house of Judah" (Jer 31:31). This passage speaks to the understanding of Jesus' death on the cross as well as to the meaning and purpose of the Eucharist. At its foundation, the death of Jesus is a renewal of the covenant that had been made with

Israel in the past. This new covenant reestablishes the bond relationship that exists between God and a new people through the death of Jesus on the cross, through the shedding of his blood.

The Spirit and the Body of Christ

Prior to the account of the institution of the Eucharist, Paul draws out the implications of our participation in the Eucharist when he says, "I am speaking as to sensible people; judge for yourselves what I am saying. The cup of blessing that we bless, is it not a participation in the blood of Christ? The bread that we break, is it not a participation in the body of Christ? Because the loaf of bread is one, we, though many, are one body, for we all partake of the one loaf" (1 Cor 10:15-17). This is a wonderful description of the relationship that emerges from one's participation in the Body and Blood of Christ. Through the power of the Spirit, one is brought into relationship with the risen Christ and at the same time into relationship with everyone else who shares in this celebration. As one's body needs sustenance to support itself daily, so the Body of Christ sustains one's life spiritually. At the same time, the risen Christ draws all people into unity with him, and each one becomes part of his Body. Pope Benedict XVI expresses this thought insightfully, "If man eats ordinary bread, in the digestive process this bread becomes part of his body, transformed into a substance of human life. But in holy Communion the inverse process is brought about. Christ, the Lord, assimilates us into himself, introducing us into his glorious Body, and thus we all become his Body."[6]

In 1 Corinthians 12 and Romans 12, Paul uses eucharistic language in order to draw out the implications of our relationship as the Body of Christ. This bond with Christ brings with it serious implications and obligations for our interaction with all members of the Body of Christ. The context of much of these two chapters involves Paul addressing conflicts and dissension within the Christian communities of Corinth and Rome to whom he is writing, respectively.

In 1 Corinthians 12, Paul addresses the tensions that have arisen within the community from the diversity of the spiritual gifts believers are experiencing. Paul reminds the community that this diversity of gifts stems from the same Spirit and the same Lord, "There are different kinds of spiritual gifts but the same Spirit; there are different forms of service but the same Lord" (12:4-5). In this context some members of the community are causing dissension by claiming a superiority for their gifts over those of others. To counter this arrogance, Paul uses the image of the Body of Christ to show that just as a human body is made up of different members, the same is true of the Body of Christ, "Now the body is not a single part, but many"(12:14). Each member has a particular function and role to fulfill, and each member within the Body of Christ must also respect and value all the other members: "If a foot should say, 'Because I am not a hand I do not belong to the body,' it does not for this reason belong any less to the body" (12:15). This respect and honor given to each member within the body should lead to concern for the needs of each member as well, "If [one] part suffers, all the parts suffer with it; if one part is honored, all the parts share its joy" (12:26).

The major spiritual teaching that emerges from Paul's discussion here is the stress he places on the importance and equality of every person within the Body of Christ. While there is a diversity of gifts, each gift is essential for building up the community and the Body of Christ. Each member makes a contribution in his or her way to the whole Body of Christ. Paul's message is equally important for us and for our spirituality in the twenty-first century. Our relationship with Christ is not simply an individual, personal relationship. It is also a community-oriented relationship. Through the one Spirit, we are all brought together as members in the Body of Christ. This brings with it a responsibility and concern for every member of this Body. Ours is the task to build up this Body by using those gifts with which the Spirit graced us. No one is more important than anyone else in the Body of Christ. The diversity of gifts that make up the Body are essential for the proper functioning of the Body.

Spiritual Worship

An important dimension of one's spirituality is how worship rejuvenates one's life. Union with Christ through the Spirit transforms the worship one now offers to God. This worship is possible only through Christ and is offered to God though our living bodies. Paul's spirituality reveals two significant points in this regard. In the first place, the transformed worship embraces a union with the person of Christ Jesus; second, it involves a worship that is offered through our living beings.

Worship in Union with Christ Jesus

All have sinned and are deprived of the glory of God. They are justified freely by God's grace through the redemption in Christ Jesus, whom God set forth as an expiation, through faith, by his blood, to prove his righteousness because of the forgiveness of sins previously committed. . . . (Rom 3:23-25)

Paul indicates here that while worship previously had centered on the temple in Jerusalem, now it is transformed through a worship centered on Jesus in his death on the cross. Paul refers to "the expiation" or "the propitiatory," which is a technical term the people of Israel used to refer to the cover of the ark of the covenant that was in the most holy place in the temple of Jerusalem. The Israelites believed this *propitiatory* was the place of contact between God and humanity. From here God dispensed divine blessings on God's people. Their worship was directed toward this seat of God. On the Day of Atonement (*Yom Kippur*) the high priest entered this sacred area and sprinkled animal blood on this seat as a way of asking God to remove the sins of the people of Israel.

Now, the person of Jesus Christ on the cross has become the new *propitiatory* and, through his blood, has taken away the sins of humanity. Jesus Christ on the cross became the place of contact between God and humanity, and it is from this cross God dispensed God's blessings, forgiveness, and salvation for all humanity. In a symbolic way, the old worship has given way to a new worship. The old worship was focused on a place, the temple of Jerusalem. The new worship is focused on a person, Jesus Christ. The love of God for humanity as demonstrated in the very death of his Son on the cross replaces a worship centered on the death of animals. Love is what animates this new worship, a worship that embraces the very center of one's being, one's spirit.

From the perspective of spirituality, the real significance here is that worship has been transformed from worship centered on a place to worship centered on a person, the person of Jesus Christ. Further, this new spiritual worship is founded upon the death and resurrection of Christ.

A Living Sacrifice, a Spiritual Worship

> I urge you therefore, brothers, by the mercies of God, to offer your bodies as a living sacrifice, holy and pleasing to God, your spiritual worship. Do not conform yourselves to this age but be transformed by the renewal of your mind, that you may discern what is the will of God, what is good and pleasing and perfect. (Rom 12:1-2)

This verse sets forth the identity of a Christian as well as how that identity provides the foundation for a Christian way of life. Two phrases are significant in this regard: "a living sacrifice" and a "spiritual worship."

In the context of this verse, Paul calls on his hearers to "present your bodies as a living sacrifice." Christians are called to offer their bodies in worship to God. The body refers in the Hebrew sense to one's whole being. God is to be worshiped in one's whole being, one's totality. We can understand Paul's thought here if we refer to what he says else-where where he draws out his insights more deliberately: "Do you not know that your body is a temple of the holy Spirit within you, whom you have from God, and that you are not your own? For you have been purchased at a price. Therefore, glorify God in your body" (1 Cor 6:19-20). Through Jesus' death on the cross we have, as it were, been purchased by Christ. The power of the Spirit has communicated to us the effects of his death, and our sins are taken away. The Spirit dwells within us transforming us into "temple(s) of the Holy Spirit." We are able to worship God in our bodies by leading a life that gives glory and honor to God through our daily actions. Every aspect of our lives becomes a way of praising God. What an amazing insight!

When we hear Paul speak of "a living sacrifice," our minds are brought back to the sacrificial language of the Old Testament. The term sacrifice conjures up images of the animal sacrifices in the temple of Jerusalem whereby an animal is killed and then burned on the altar as an offering to God. However, Paul says something paradoxical in this passage when he speaks of a "living sacrifice." Paul is in effect making a connection to a tradition that was well expressed in Psalm 51:

> For you do not desire sacrifice or I would give it;
> a burnt offering you would not accept.
> My sacrifice, O God, is a contrite spirit;
> a contrite, humbled heart, O God, you will not scorn. (51:18-19)

The same thoughts are expressed by the prophets, as Isaiah says at the beginning of his prophecies,

> What do I care for the multitude of your sacrifices?
> says the LORD.
> I have had enough of whole-burnt rams
> and fat of fatlings. . .
> Wash yourselves clean! (Isa 1:11, 16; see also Amos 5:21-22;
> Hos 6:6)

This tradition on which Paul draws stresses that sacrifices in them-selves are worthless unless they come from a heart that is filled with the right intentions. One must lead a life in dedication to God, in a spirit of sincerity to God, and in obedience to the teachings of God.

Paul's contribution to this tradition is to add that true worship can be accomplished only in union with Christ Jesus and our association with his death on the cross. On one's own one is unable to offer to God the pure sacrifice that God is calling upon Christians to offer. Only "in Christ" are Christians truly able to become a living sacrifice, a sacrifice united with the whole Body of Christ. After all, the only true sacrifice is the one offered in Christ. The doxology of the eucharistic prayer prays, "Through him, and with him, and in him . . . all glory and honor is yours. . . ." In his sacrifice, Jesus Christ, through his humanity, takes us together with him in offering himself to the Father. We unite ourselves with his offering and in this way become a "living sacrifice" to the Father.

In another instance, Eucharistic Prayer I reflects Paul's reference to this spiritual worship when it says, "Be pleased, O God, we pray, to bless, acknowledge, and approve this offering in every respect; make it spiritual [in Latin *rationabilem*] and acceptable, so that it may become for us the Body and Blood of your most beloved Son, our Lord Jesus Christ." Pope Benedict explains how the Church has interpreted these words of Paul about becoming a living sacrifice:

> The Church knows that in the Holy Eucharist Christ's gift of himself, his true sacrifice, becomes present. However, the Church prays that the community celebrating may truly be united with Christ and transformed; she prays that we may become what we cannot be with our own efforts: a "rational" offering that is acceptable to God. Thus the Eucharistic Prayer interprets Saint Paul's words correctly.[7]

Identity Shapes Ethical Action

Following Paul's call for the Christian life to be "a living sacrifice . . . spiritual worship" (Rom 12:1), the rest of the letter to the Romans illustrates the action that this way of life should adopt. Since you are "a living sacrifice," Paul goes on to say, "Do not conform yourselves to this age but be transformed by the renewal of your mind" (12:2). One must not simply avoid the ways of the world—one's mindset, one's identity as a person, has been transformed through being in Christ. As part of the Body of Christ, one's life is led in imitation of the way Jesus Christ led his life. Through the power of the Spirit that dwells within us, our values have been transformed. As part of the Body of Christ and guided by the Spirit, a new perspective is brought to bear on every action. In Romans, Paul gives some thirty imperatives that are all guided by the basic law of love, "Let love be sincere; hate what is evil, hold on to what is good; love one another with mutual affection; anticipate one another in showing honor" (12:9-10). The values emanating from love demand concern for those in need. Paul calls upon his readers to demonstrate affection and empathy for everyone.

Paul reveals a principle evident in all his letters that identity must influence action: who we are (the *indicative*) leads to what we must do (the *imperative*). Identity leads to a corresponding moral action. Since you are a living sacrifice (*indicative*), therefore you must lead your life in a specific way (*imperative*). Without doubt this is the motor that drives Paul's spirituality: the awareness that since we have become a new creation through the death and resurrection of Christ we must now respond with a life that reflects this identity. In living out our identity, we have the power of the Spirit within us enabling us to lead life as "a new creation in Christ."

Love is the central virtue of Paul's spirituality because it lies at the foundation of Jesus' whole life story as well as that of Paul. The true expression of love is captured in the cross of Christ. Paul portrays the clearest example of this love of Christ in his hymn in Philippians 2:6-11. This is the true paradigm of the self-giving love of Christ that is meant to be imitated by all believers. This hymn has already been addressed, but what is significant to note in this context is Paul's call to have the same mindset as that of Christ Jesus, who emptied himself and humbled himself out of love for humanity. Paul introduced the hymn in Philippians by issuing a call to imitate the self-emptying love of Christ:

> If there is any encouragement in Christ, any solace in love, any participation in the Spirit, any compassion and mercy, complete my joy by being of the same mind, with the same love, united in heart, thinking one thing. Do nothing from selfishness or out of vainglory; rather, humbly regard others as more important than yourselves, each looking out not for his own interests, but [also] everyone for those of others. (Phil 2:1-4)

Paul challenges the community by indicating that the pattern of Jesus' life story should become their own. They should move away from self-interest to embrace humility and a genuine concern for the welfare of others just as Jesus emptied himself and embraced death on behalf of humanity. Worth noting here is that Paul's ethical teaching does not set forth a series of rules for determining exactly what one has to do. Paul's approach is rather to invite his communities to take seriously the paradigm of the cross and resurrection of Christ. Each believer and each community will discern the response to the challenges each faces on the basis of the cruciform love of Christ Jesus. Believers are to imitate the cruciform love of Christ in every situation of life.

Paul illustrates this cruciform love in his own life by living, as he says, "within the law of Christ" (1 Cor 9:21). He endeavors to "become all things to all, to save at least some" (9:22). Just as Christ humbled himself by taking on human nature and becoming obedient to death, so too Paul shows he has given up much in order to identify himself with those with whom he strives to share the gospel. In our own lives, the paradigm of the story of Christ (namely, his humiliation, obedience to death, and identification with us as human beings) should be how we approach all the situations of life. Ours should be the path where we identify with others and are willing to empathize with them to the extent that we walk in their shoes and bring the love of Christ to them in their situations. That is the essence of Paul's spiritual way of life.

Insights for Our Own Spiritual Journey: Community-Oriented Spirituality

Life of the Spirit

The great contribution Paul has made, as is evident from the reflections in this chapter, is that the foundation and source of all spirituality for the Christian lies in "the life of the *Spirit*." The Spirit transforms our human spirit so that in experiencing the grace that stems from the cross and resurrection of Christ we are given the power to be able to lead our lives in imitation of Christ Jesus. More than any other writer in the New Testament, Paul gives attention to the role of the Spirit in the lives of believers as well as within the life of the community. Both Paul and his communities are familiar with the presence of God's Spirit in their lives. Their understanding of the Spirit comes not through intellectual debate but through real, personal experience. In the sacraments of baptism and the Eucharist, they celebrate the power of God's Spirit. Their identity as followers of Jesus Christ is attributable to the Spirit's power working in their lives. God's Spirit is the very source of their identity as Christians and as a Christian community, as the Body of Christ. The Spirit is the spiritual force that transforms the human spirit, making it possible for every believer to live the cruciform life she or he is called to live.

Above all, the gifts of the Holy Spirit are intended for the building up of the community. Paul's spirituality shows that God's working in our lives not only transforms our lives but redirects our spirituality to others. There is no such thing as a spirituality that is individualistic in the sense that it creates an elite separation from the community. One bears a responsibility to make a contribution to the world in which one lives.

Our spirituality is enlivened through the sacraments. Through them we experience more intensely the life of the Spirit. The Catholic imagination is a sacramental imagination that sees God working in the world and in nature. Nature and grace work together. As Andrew Greeley expresses it, "I have tried to explain what I think the Catholic imagination is, namely, one that views the world and all that is in it as enchanted, haunted by the Holy Spirit and the presence of grace."[8] In the simple actions of washing and in eating a meal, God's Spirit is present, transforming the lives of those washed in the waters of baptism and given the bread so they may become the Body of Christ. These transformations of the elements of creation now touch the lives of believers, who in turn are transformed in their journey of life. Such a spirituality views the world as God's playground, where God brings joy and peace to the lives of those who believe, who see the world through the eyes of the Spirit. After all, Paul tells us that no one can pray unless the Spirit prays through them. The Spirit opens our eyes, our imagination, to see the world through God's eyes.

Paul's spirituality adds to the Catholic imagination by enabling one to see the cross and resurrection of Christ as the way to lead one's life. In the celebration of the Eucharist, this reminder is continued, as Paul reminds his readers, "For as often as you eat this bread and drink the cup, you proclaim the death of the Lord until he comes" (1 Cor 11:26). Imagination helps realize that celebration of the Eucharist unites believers with Christ's death and resurrection. Not only do we imagine it, but through the power of the Spirit we experience in our own lives the effects of Jesus' death and resurrection—they are communicated to us. The Spirit touches our own spirits, our imaginations, as well as the very essence of our beings. We are called as well to live out what we experience in the celebration of the sacraments. We too must embrace the cross in our lives and in doing so we know that we will eventually experience the resurrection.

A Community-Oriented Spirituality: The Body of Christ

In the celebration of the ritual of baptism a wonderful symbolic action takes place after the actual baptism. The one baptized puts on a white garment as the minister says:

> You have become a new creation, and have clothed yourself in Christ. See in this white garment the outward sign of your Christian dignity. With your family and friends to help you by word and example bring that dignity unstained into the everlasting life of heaven.

"Clothed yourself in Christ": These words are a reminder of Paul's call to his fellow Christians to "Put on the Lord Jesus Christ" (Rom 13:14). Paul urges his readers, as they put on their garments, to put on Christ, to turn away from their former lives as they now enter a new community, the Body of Christ. "Let us then throw off the works of darkness, [and] put on the armor of light; let us conduct ourselves properly as in the day, not in orgies and drunkenness, not in promiscuity and licentiousness, not in rivalry and jealousy. But put on the Lord Jesus Christ, and make no provision for the desires of the flesh" (Rom 13:12-14). These are the words Augustine read when he had his dramatic conversion in the garden of Milan. As in the life of Augustine, Paul's spirituality stresses that God works within us to transform our lives. The Lord gives us the spiritual strength we need to avoid those desires and evil tendencies pulling us away from God. If there is one thing that is central for us in Paul's spirituality, it is the reminder that on our own we cannot accomplish anything; it is always the grace of God's Spirit working within us, enabling us to transcend our human weakness. The symbolic gesture of putting on a white garment in baptism is a graphic image that demonstrates visually this central spiritual truth: allow Christ to clothe and transform me to become a new creation, a temple of God's Spirit, purified from every trace of sin, and a productive member of the Body of Christ.

Paul's spirituality is above all centered around and oriented to a community, the Body of Christ. The gifts of the Spirit are given to individuals not for themselves alone, but for the building up of the Body of Christ. As Paul says, "To each individual the manifestation of the Spirit is given *for some benefit*" (1 Cor 12:7; italics added). He goes on to speak about the different spiritual gifts (*charismata*) the Spirit communicates, among which he lists prophecy, ministry, teaching, healing, speaking in tongues, and interpretation of tongues (12:7-11). Not all gifts are the same. The grace of God's Spirit unleashes within each of us certain human abilities. Together they create the diverse community of the Body of Christ.

By the grace of God's Spirit, one comes to realize his or her strengths and weaknesses. No one person has all the gifts. The Spirit helps one recognize and realize one's potentials and actualize one's abilities. Paul's spirituality is realistic about our humanity. It celebrates our strengths, but also accepts our limitations. The Spirit communicates the gifts of shalom, the gifts of living at peace with oneself and in one's relationships with God and with others.

As a new creation in Christ, each one of us forms part of the Body of Christ. This means that our spirituality is other centered. This spirituality is such that each person strives to build up the Body of Christ: "Now the body is not a single part, but many . . . If the whole body were an eye, where would the hearing be?" (1 Cor 12:14, 17). One's abilities and spiritual gifts are there to help others; they are for the common good. On the other hand, one must also acknowledge one's own limitations to build up the body of Christ.

An Ethical Spirituality: Identity Shapes Action

In Paul's spiritualty, the Body of Christ is where the love of Christ is experienced. Within the context of the community of the Body of Christ, one discerns the needs of the community and responds to them with love. Paul's spirituality, expressed in a moral way of life, is directed exclusively by the principle (as already noted) that the *indicative* leads to the *imperative*. In other words, the indicative is the reality that I have put on Christ, "I live no longer I, but Christ lives in me." This is my identity and I lead my life accordingly. The foundational understanding of the life of Paul is that he led his life not for himself but for others. Love for the other is the essence of Paul's spirituality. Paul did not give a set of rules or regulations to be followed legalistically. What he did give was a way of living in imitation of the person of Christ. Paul knows as well that moral laws cannot answer every question. The one path that offers an answer to every question is the way of the love of Christ who humbled himself to death for the sake of humanity.

Paul illustrates this approach in the dispute about eating meat offered to idols (1 Cor 8:1–9:27). Paul states categorically that idols do not exist, "We know that 'there is no idol in the world,' and that 'there is no God but one'" (1 Cor 8:4). However, Paul recognizes that for some people used to worshipping idols, their conscience is so weak that they are scandalized if someone were to eat such meat. Paul concludes that the better thing to do in such a situation is to abstain from eating that meat since it is a cause of scandal to others. "Therefore, if food causes my brother to sin, I will never eat meat again, so that I may not cause my brother to sin" (1 Cor 8:13). Here is a very significant aspect of Paul's spirituality: there are times when one needs to forgo one's rights in order to serve the good of the other person. In the Body of Christ, we do not demand rights and dues. Instead, through service of others, we strive to build up the Body of Christ. How can the Body of Christ be strengthened if one insists upon one's own rights? This runs counter to the love of Christ.

Paul illustrates this further in his own life where he says that as an apostle he has certain rights, chief among them is to be supported by those to whom he preaches the Gospel. "Do we not have the right to eat and drink? Do we not have the right to take along a Christian wife, as do the rest of the apostles, and the brothers of the Lord, and Cephas?" (1 Cor 9:4-5). However, despite having declared such rights, Paul says that he has forgone those rights because he does not want to be a burden upon the community. Paul lays out the way of life he has decided to follow: "When I preach, I offer the gospel free of charge so as not to make full use of my right in the gospel. Although I am free in regard to all, I have made myself a slave to all so as to win over as many as possible" (1 Cor 9:18-19). By making himself a slave to all and putting aside his rights, Paul is emulating the self-sacrificing cruciform love of Christ Jesus.

Most noteworthy about Paul's spirituality is that he does not set forth his way of leading the Christian life as mandatory for everyone. In this instance, he shows clearly how the apostle has a right to receive recompense for services to the community. However, for Paul his spirituality leads him along another path, the path that imitates the selfless service and cruciform love of Christ.

The Goal of the Spiritual Life

"For just as in Adam all die, so too in Christ shall all be brought to life."

(1 Cor 15:22)

An Eschatological Spirituality

With the resurrection of Jesus, the early Christians believed the end times had already begun. The future resurrection had broken into our world. Throughout this examination of Paul's spirituality we have seen that the death and resurrection of Jesus were at its very foundation. Paul quotes the tradition that had been handed on to him and which in effect was one of the earliest creeds, or professions of faith, of the early Christian community:

> For I handed on to you as of first importance what I also received: that Christ died for our sins in accordance with the scriptures; that he was buried; that he was raised on the third day in accordance with the scriptures; that he appeared to Cephas, then to the Twelve.
> (1 Cor 15:3-5)

Paul has in mind the tradition coming from the Christian community and the other apostles. Paul is also heir to another tradition, namely, one coming from Israel, from the Old Testament. Paul never abandoned his Jewish heritage and its traditions. His belief in Christ Jesus enabled him to view his Jewish traditions with new insights and interpretation. The same is true with regard to the eschatological tradition. Literally the word *eschatology,* derived from two Greek words *eschaton* (last, final, end) and *logos* (word), means a word or a study about the end times. Eschatology, then, is a discussion of "the last things," the end of world. The people of Israel at the time of Paul were looking forward expectantly to the accomplishment of God's plan for the world, a plan that had been unfolding slowly in the words of the prophets over the centuries. Central to this future world would be God's unexpected intervention to restore God's kingdom, where evil would be punished and good would be rewarded. A great destruction would occur with the overthrow of kingdoms and nations, and the world would be transformed into one oriented toward God's will. These hopes and thoughts that were addressed largely in symbolic images and vocabulary (as can be seen in the books of Daniel and Revelation) are referred to as "apocalyptic eschatology." The word "apocalyptic" (from the Greek word *apokalypsis* meaning revelation) refers to the revelation or making known of the last things, the end times.

When Jesus was raised from the dead, Christians saw this as proof that these "end times" had already arrived. Since the rest of the hopes of the people of Israel did not materialize, Jesus' followers interpreted these events as taking place in two stages. The resurrection of Jesus from the dead initiated the first phase of God's plan for the salvation for the world. The final stage had been postponed until later when Jesus, the Messiah,[1] would return and the judgment of the nations of the world would take place with the separation of the good from the evil. At that time all people would experience the resurrection of the dead as Jesus Christ had already experienced.

The simple statement of Paul and all the apostles that "God had raised Jesus from the dead" was a way of saying the age of the Messiah had begun. Paul's thought is to be understood in this context. For Paul, the resurrection was not an isolated event to be understood on its own. The resurrection of Jesus is an indication that what has happened to Jesus will happen to all in the age to come. It is a foretaste of what is in store for those who believe. Jesus is the "first fruits" of the resurrection, as Paul says in 1 Corinthians:

> But now Christ has been raised from the dead, the firstfruits of those who have fallen asleep. For since death came through a human being, the resurrection of the dead came also through a human being. For just as in Adam all die, so too in Christ shall all be brought to life. . . . (15:20-22)

Expressed simply, a *future* event (Jesus' resurrection) broke into the *past* as an assurance to us *now* of our own *future* resurrection. Biblical scholars speak about this sense of past, present and future in terms of "already" (Latin: *iam*) and "not yet" (Latin: *nondum*). We are *already* living in the eschatological age (since Christ has experienced the resurrection) while on the other hand we are *not yet* in the final end times when all will be changed and transformed in the resurrection of the dead.

Perhaps this way of speaking sounds strange: already/not yet, or "the future has already burst into our past and gives meaning to our present." An analogy or story might illustrate this language more easily:

> Your sister returned last year from a vacation in Italy. She had such an amazing time and told you and your family all about it: the holy places and historical sites she visited, the glorious weather, the abundance of great wine and food, and the highlight of her trip— seeing the Holy Father, Pope Francis. She was so excited about her experience. Her excitement was contagious! She convinced your whole family to visit Italy the next summer. You planned for it by viewing the pictures your sister took and researching all the places you were to visit. You went ahead and booked the plane tickets as well as the hotels where you would be staying. Your whole experience leading up to your departure is similar to this "already" and "not yet." Her past experiences, excitement, and enthusiasm generate within you a foretaste for what you are going to experience when you go there. As you approach your own travel to Italy, you are *already* living in expectation of what you are going to experience; *"the future has already burst into your life and is giving meaning to your present."* Your preparations for your travels show that you are *already* living now in anticipation of your future trip, while at the same time you are *not yet* there.

This example demonstrates the meaning behind one saying that eschatology has *already* begun with the resurrection of Jesus. We live now in an age of anticipation for the future when we too will experience the resurrection from the dead. We are *not yet* there. Christ's resurrection (your sister's *past* trip to Italy) gives insight into what you will experience in the resurrection of the dead (your *future* experiences in Italy). As a Christian, you lead your life following the teachings and message of Jesus in anticipation of your future life with God (just as you *now* plan your travel in anticipation of what you hope to experience in your own trip). *Past* and *future* all come together in the *present now.* The resurrection of Jesus influences our present and gives us the foretaste of our future life with God. This is what is meant by an "eschatological spirituality."

The experience of the gift of the Spirit was further support for the early believers' conviction of their hopes for the future resurrected life. Just as Paul's experience of the risen Jesus on the road to Damascus convinced him of the reality of Jesus' resurrection, so too the experience of the Spirit in Paul's life and the lives of fellow members in his communities convinced Paul and his communities that the future life with God was already being experienced in their present. Paul expresses this conviction when he speaks of their experience of the Spirit: "But the one who gives us security with you in Christ and who anointed us is God; he has also put his seal upon us and given the Spirit in our hearts as a first installment" (2 Cor 1:21-22). This is a remarkable trinitarian statement: God the Father has brought us together through baptism in Christ and has stamped us with a seal that claims us as his own by means of the Spirit that has been communicated to us. The Spirit is referred to as "the first installment," as a type of "down payment" we have received. The gifts of the Spirit are a foretaste of what we are to experience in the future life with God.

The outpouring of the Spirit was a central part of the eschatological hopes of Israel. For the first Christians, the outpouring of the Spirit was a sign that the messianic age had begun. As a "first installment" it was simply a foretaste of what was in store for all Christians. Paul also refers to the Spirit dwelling within the believer as proof that we will be raised to eternal life. The presence of the Spirit in our lives is testimony to this belief: "If the Spirit of the one who raised Jesus from the dead dwells in you, the one who raised Christ from the dead will give life to your mortal bodies also, through his Spirit that dwells in you" (Rom 8:11).

Although Paul never uses the word eschatology in his letters, he does show his awareness of the rich Israelite apocalyptic tradition in a number of texts. He gives attention to the present age as a time of struggle against the forces of evil. It is a period before the coming of Christ when those who were faithful would experience salvation and those who had done evil would be punished. Paul speaks of this coming of Christ as the *parousia* (a Greek word that means *arrival* or *coming*): "For just as in Adam all die, so too in Christ shall all be brought to life, but each one in the proper order: Christ the firstfruits; then at his coming [*parousia*], those who belong to Christ; then comes the end, when he hands over the kingdom to his God and Father, when he has destroyed every sovereignty and every authority and power" (1 Cor 15:22-24).

Elsewhere, Paul uses the striking apocalyptic language to describe the coming of the "Day of the Lord": "For the Lord himself, with a word of command, with the voice of an archangel and with the trumpet of God, will come down from heaven, and the dead in Christ will rise first. Then we who are alive, who are left, will be caught up together with them in the clouds to meet the Lord in the air. Thus we shall always be with the Lord" (1 Thess 4:16-17). The images of clouds, voices of angels, and a trumpet are not intended to give a literal account of what will happen. Instead, Paul wishes to express, by means of imagery, what ultimately is a mystery. As Pope Benedict wrote, "Paul describes Christ's *parousia* in especially vivid tones and with symbolic imagery which, however, conveys a simple and profound message: we shall ultimately be with the Lord forever. Over and above the images, this is the essential message: our future is 'to be with the Lord.'"[2]

Central in Paul's spirituality is his commitment to lead life with the expectation that union with Christ that has already begun and that is empowered by the Spirit will continue into the future. Death is simply a passageway from this life to the life with God forever. The relationship one experiences with Christ at the present moment is one that will reach fullness and completion in the future life with God. This conviction influences Paul's whole life, and it explains the serenity that permeates everything that happens to him. For example, Paul writes his letter to the Philippians from prison, where he does not know what will happen to him: he is faced with death or with being released. In weighing up both possibilities, Paul shows he willingly accepts whatever will happen though he makes it clear which possibility he would prefer: "For to me life is Christ, and death is gain. If I go on living in the flesh, that means fruitful labor for me. And I do not know what I shall choose. I am caught between the two. I long to depart this life and be with Christ, [for] that is far better. Yet that I remain [in] the flesh is more necessary for your benefit" (Phil 1:21-24). He is following the example of Christ Jesus whose whole life was led for others. To live for others is the hallmark of Paul's life and mission. He is always open to carrying out God's plan whatever it may be. He is at the service of God and of humanity.

Paul's letter to the Philippians also contains indications of his eschatological insights and beliefs. These are found in the hymn to Christ (Phil 2:6-11). Instead of using the word *eschatology*, Paul prefers to use another term, *exaltation*, to express the same insight in a different way. In the hymn that Paul adapts from Christian worship, he describes that Christ Jesus humbled himself to become one of us but that his humiliation went even further to dying on the cross, "he humbled himself / becoming obedient to death, / even death on a cross" (2:8). What is noteworthy is that after mentioning his death on a cross, Paul speaks about Christ's exaltation, "Because of this, God greatly exalted him / and bestowed on him the name / that is above every name . . ." (2:9).

This shows that another way Paul spoke of the resurrection of Christ was to speak about "the exaltation of Christ." The exaltation of Jesus

Christ as Lord, a title that was used for God throughout the Old Testament, is also a term that is used to refer to the Roman emperor. In writing to largely Gentile-Christian readers, who would be familiar with this context, Paul describes Jesus Christ as being raised above all the powers of the universe and proclaimed as Lord of the universe. As a result of God's exaltation, Jesus Christ is established as the sovereign ruler of the universe. This language has indeed political overtones. Since the Roman emperor was lord of the people of the empire, Paul's proclamation that Jesus Christ has been established as supremely powerful was indeed a challenge: every power, whether on earth, in heaven, or under the earth, is subject to the authority and power of Jesus Christ. Paul is declaring that all earthly powers and authorities "should bend the knee" and acknowledge the sovereignty of Jesus Christ. In 1 Corinthians 15:20-28, Paul spells out more fully this rule of Christ over the universe. At the end time when Christ returns, he will overthrow every power and authority and then hand his kingdom over to the Father.

The eschatological language of resurrection expressed the teaching that, in the world to come, there will be a transformation from our earthly being and existence to a life led in union with Christ and with God. It is not just a resuscitation to another earthly existence. A new creation has emerged. In this new creation, all things are subject to the rule of Christ Jesus. The language of resurrection and exaltation capture two significant dimensions of the future life with God: on the one hand it involves a defeat (of death and sin) and a renewal; on the other hand it embraces a new relationship of power where Christ is the ruler of all, and he alone is the one to whom creation owes allegiance and worship.

Insights for Our Own Spiritual Journey: Significance of the Last Things for Our Spiritual Lives Today

A Spirituality of Joy

Paul's spirituality is by no means a spirituality that embraces a flight from the world. In fact, quite the opposite. Paul's spirituality, as shown throughout, is a lived experience of the reality of the death and resurrection of Jesus Christ.

Paul's spirituality is shaped by his firm conviction that Jesus Christ is risen. The belief that we are now living in the eschatological age shaped Paul's life and should shape ours as well. Since Jesus has overcome the forces of death through his resurrection and now rules as Lord, this belief should shape our whole daily life. Paul's life and mission is driven by his conviction that we are already living in the eschatological age and that the future has already begun. This same conviction should drive our own spiritual lives: "All of us, gazing with unveiled face on the glory of the Lord, are being transformed into the same image from glory to glory, as from the Lord who is the Spirit" (2 Cor 3:18). The process of transformation began when we were baptized and continues throughout our lives as we journey in union with Christ. Paul will also say, "You know the time; it is the hour now for you to awake from sleep. For our salvation is nearer now than when we first believed" (Rom 13:11). Our journey of life is a journey with Christ and to Christ. This provides both the motivation and the strength for leading our lives in a way that takes seriously our future belief and hope. This future hope does not instill fear in us but rather confidence and joy in what lies ahead of us.

Paul's spirituality is dominated by the spirit of joy. The letter to the Philippians is the most joyful of all of Paul's letters (the word "joy" in some form occurs sixteen times): "Rejoice in the Lord, always. I shall say it again: rejoice!" (Phil 4:4). At the same time, Paul's situation is one of suffering, of imprisonment and facing the prospect of death. In the very sufferings that Paul experiences lies his hope and certainty of a transformation in the future. In his sufferings, Paul identifies himself with the crucified Christ. He shares in the suffering of Christ that offers Paul the assurance of a future transformation. The experience of Jesus' sufferings transformed in the resurrection offers Paul and us eternal hope that the sufferings of this present time hold within themselves the assurance that reversal and glory lie at hand. Paul's spirituality offers us a hope for the future as well as the assurance that in this present eschatological age, through our sufferings, we are living a life in conformity to the image of Christ Jesus.

A Spirituality of Assurance that Jesus Christ Is with Me

Our belief that the risen Christ lives in and with each one of us through the gift of the Spirit not only gives direction for the future but also offers assurance, consolation, and hope for the present. The world today can be a very frightening place. On the world stage there are so many areas where wars are being fought, people are being killed, thousands are displaced from their homes and living in refugee camps. The news of the day is depressing. On the home front life is just as fragile: the economy over the past decade has been stagnant; many people struggle to find jobs to support themselves and their families; violence breaks out sporadically in our nation; our political leaders struggle to work together for the good of society; even families find difficulty in living together in harmony and peace. From a simple human viewpoint, the future looks bleak, and many have a real fear of the future.

With our belief and experience of the presence of Christ in our lives, life takes on a very different perspective. We approach the world we live in with a positive spirituality. The joy that Paul experienced should permeate our lives as well. Our spirituality does not expect Christ to change the situations in which we are, but our spirituality does teach us that we are not alone as we face the struggles of daily life with its uncertainties and fears. Paul's statement, "I am content with weaknesses, insults, hardships, persecutions, and constraints, for the sake of Christ; for when I am weak, then I am strong" (2 Cor 12:10), should be a reassuring reminder that the presence of Christ with one gives one the strength to face the challenges of each day. Like Paul, we are called to approach life with the firm conviction that with Christ we can face whatever obstacle comes our way. There is nothing to fear in the large scheme of things because there is a future life with God that puts an end to these earthly struggles and fears. If we live in the light of our future life with Christ and with our present belief that Christ is with us, we have now the strength and power to deal with the future.

A Spirituality of Responsibility for the World and for Our Fellow Travelers

When Paul writes to the Philippians from prison, his reflections act as an inspiration to all of us and to our own spirituality. Faced with the two possible outcomes of his imprisonment, Paul evaluated his situation in a striking way. While he would prefer to be sentenced to death and be with Christ, he saw that the Lord wanted him to continue his life journey for the sake of the Philippians and for spreading the message of Christ. Ours is the responsibility to do likewise. Following the example of Christ and of Paul, we also live our lives for others and we strive to serve and help them.

We do have a further responsibility beyond that of renewing the relationships among people. We also bear a responsibility for renewing the world in which we live. In the book of Genesis in the story of the creation of the human beings, God instructs them in this way: "God blessed them and God said to them: Be fertile and multiply; fill the earth and subdue it" (Gen 1:28). In this twofold command, God lays out the primary responsibilities for humanity: to continue the human race and to care for the planet we inhabit. "To subdue" is to be understood in the sense of exercising responsibility for the created world that God has entrusted to us.

> For creation awaits with eager expectation the revelation of the children of God; for creation was made subject to futility, not of its own accord but because of the one who subjected it, in hope that creation itself would be set free from slavery to corruption and share in the glorious freedom of the children of God. We know that all creation is groaning in labor pains even until now, and not only that, but we ourselves, who have the firstfruits of the Spirit, we also groan within ourselves as we wait for adoption, the redemption of our bodies. (Rom 8:19-23)

Paul's words show a strong connection between human beings and creation. Since sin and death affected not just the human being but creation itself, the resurrection will also involve not just the human being but creation as well. One tends to have a too narrow and individualistic understanding of the resurrection and its effects.[3] The renewal the resurrection brings will embrace humanity as well as creation. This gives an exciting new insight into a spirituality for today's world. Ordinary people today are energized by a responsibility for our world and for our environment. Paul's spirituality connects closely with the aspirations and desires of those today who want to ensure that we do not destroy our planet and that we do everything to renew it. The resurrection of Christ is proof of the future renewal of humanity and of creation itself. Through faith and the sacraments we already share in a foretaste of this renewed life. Through the grace of Christ and the Spirit we have the responsibility of working toward the renewal of humanity and of the creation in which we live. God's future actions in the transformation of humanity and the cosmos do not depend upon our contributions; nevertheless, our actions do make a difference in preparing humanity and the world for the future coming of Christ.

Our spirituality today is energized by Paul's insights into our hope for the renewal of all things in Christ. Peace, justice, and harmony will be restored to a fragmented world, fragmented relationships among people, and a fragmented experience of oneself. These hopes shape our spirituality and inspire us to work toward the renewal of our world as well as the lives of our fellow travelers.

Belief in the resurrection of Christ is the foundation for our whole life's spiritual journey. The inspiration that life has been renewed in Christ enables one to see that spirituality is not confined only to the realm of oneself individualistically. Rather, it brings with it an insight that one is not content with a salvation that is confined only to oneself and one's own aspirations. Spirituality embraces the need for sharing one's vision with others, in working for their good and for the welfare of others and also in building up the world in which one lives: to bring peace, justice, and harmony and to renew the cosmos itself. This spirituality also embraces working with others who are striving for the renewal of all things. As Virginia Wiles expresses it so beautifully:

> The revelation of God in Christ is a revelation of God's ultimate renewal of the entire cosmos. Faith is the confidence that, in Christ, God has revealed the truth about God and about humanity. Faith means living in the now, based on that Aha! moment of grace in the past. Hope is the extension of this confidence into the future—not only for ourselves but for the whole of creation.[4]

Paul concludes his first letter to the Corinthians with the prayer, *"Marana tha,"* which is an Aramaic phrase for "O Lord, Come!" (1 Cor 16:22). The book of Revelation has a similar prayer in Greek, "Amen! Come, Lord Jesus!" (Rev 22:20). These words were probably liturgical prayers expressing the hopes that the return of the Lord would be soon. We may not pray today for the end of the world. What we do pray for is an end to the evils that occur in our world: an end to the genocide that happens so frequently in different parts of our world, an end to wars, an end to human trafficking that is a modern form of slavery, an end to the abuse of children, and an end to so many other evils that threaten our society and our world. Our spirituality today is inspired by this prayer in that not only do we pray for an end to these evils, we also work toward ending these evils for humanity. Inspired by our prayers and our faith, our lives respond with an energy that works toward renewing our own lives and the lives of those around us. In everything we do, our starting point always remains the presence of Christ in us and with us. Renewed in the life of Christ's grace and the Spirit of God, we strive to bring Christ's presence into our society and our world.

Part Three

Paul's Spirituality
Incarnate and Alive Today

Over the past twenty-one centuries, Paul's spiritual vision has continued to enliven, transform, and challenge the Christian church. Ideas and themes from Paul's spirituality have continued to serve as an inspiration to Christians as they endeavor to live out faithfully the gospel message of Jesus Christ. Every age has appropriated Paul's spiritual vision in ways that make it relevant to their world and to their age.

This final section brings together some major spiritual themes that have emerged from our journey through Paul's spirituality, themes that are meaningful for us living in the twenty-first century. In addition to capturing the significance of each theme for our world today, this chapter also offers examples of individuals whose lives illustrated and were informed by these themes from Paul's spirituality. Without doubt a person's life is the most effective and authentic way to illustrate the significance and vitality of this spiritual vision.

Paul's Spirituality for Today

"For those who live according to the flesh set their minds on the things of the flesh, but those who live according to the Spirit set their minds on the things of the Spirit. To set the mind on the flesh is death, but to set the mind on the Spirit is life and peace."

(Rom 8:5-6, NRSV)

Paul's spirituality is based upon his encounter and experience of the risen Christ. As a Hebrew believer in God's committed relationship with the people of Israel in the covenant, Paul could not accept initially that Jesus was the Messiah, the greatest obstacle being Jesus' crucifixion. Paul's encounter with the risen Christ transformed his whole life. Through his reflections on the Scriptures as well as the traditions of his people, Paul came to see the cross in a totally new light.

Paul's response to his experience of and newfound faith in the risen Jesus brought him to see his life and faith in a new light and this transformed his spirituality. From a human point of view, we all know how our ways of thinking influence our lives. If one has a positive mindset, one is more likely to be a joyful and happy person and to see life in a positive and affirming way. If one has a pessimistic outlook on life, one is more likely to be despondent and look upon oneself and one's place in the world as a victim who always gets a raw deal in life. Our spiritual way of thinking also has a very real way of influencing our lives. As Paul says, "For those who live according to the flesh are concerned with the things of the flesh, but those who live according to the Spirit with the things of the Spirit" (Rom 8:5).[1]

Society trains us to look upon our world and upon others from a purely human perspective. Simply watch the news and ask yourself this question: "How are people being assessed?" One immediately realizes that the focus is on success: values are distorted; love and sexuality are interchangeable; people are manipulated, ridiculed and treated as objects. Paul's spirituality teaches one to view people from a different mindset: they are human beings, not only made in the image of God, but transformed into new creations through the death of Christ. When we view life "according to the Spirit," we see people and events with a completely different vision, the vision of love.

Paul's approach to his faith and spirituality inspires our own approach as well. Certainly Paul lived at a different time period and within a totally different cultural world. We cannot and are not meant to become "another Paul." The challenges and problems we face are very different. However, what is significant for us living in the twenty-first century is to look to Paul's spirituality as a way in which we can respond with our faith to new challenges and difficulties that face our contemporary world and faith. We can think with Paul as we look at the challenges facing us and our own commitment to Christ. Using the same pillars of faith and spirituality that were foundational for Paul, we can respond authentically as Christians and develop a spirituality that we could call a Pauline spirituality for today.

Just as Paul's spirituality grew and developed over time, so too does our own spirituality. When we look back over our lives, we see that where we are in our relationship with God, Christ, and others has developed and changed given the different circumstances and events that we have experienced in our lives. Paul shows us that we need to have a firm center of beliefs and convictions that shape our actions. If we do not have such a core, we tend to respond sporadically to our experiences and ultimately tend to go around in circles. If I am to grow or develop as a human person, I need convictions based upon my faith and my spiritual vision of life.

If we are to take the person of Paul seriously, we need to realize that his life was shaped first of all by his faith, his belief in the covenant relationship that God had initiated with God's people. These convictions shaped Paul's spiritual life as he noted in the letter to the Philippians where he acknowledged he was "a Hebrew of Hebrew parentage, in observance of the law a Pharisee, in zeal I persecuted the church, in righteousness based on the law I was blameless" (Phil 3:5-6). Then he changed through the grace of Christ and this new spiritual vision shaped his spirituality and pointed his way of life in a new direction. Paul's example gives us direction for our own lives. For example, as a Catholic Christian one must continually ask oneself, "What does this actually mean for me?" "How does this belief shape the spiritual life I lead?" To be an authentic follower of Christ, one needs to allow one's convictions, one's faith in the risen Christ, to shape one's own response to Christ in the daily circumstances of life. In essence it is this belief of a Catholic Christian that gives shape to his or her spirituality.

Paul's spirituality, his spiritual vision on life, is without doubt founded on, formed by, guided, and directed by his faith in the risen Christ. His response to his faith, his spirituality, developed through his reflection on his experiences. He lived out his spirituality in the midst of believers and nonbelievers alike. His spirituality did not arise from a systematic development of logical thought. Rather, his spirituality developed from the questions his communities posed to him (as in the first letter to the Corinthians) as well as the problems he encountered in the lives of communities that he had founded and who were struggling with issues related to their Christian faith. The guidance and direction Paul offered his communities were based upon certain foundational pillars that were central to his belief.

In the course of this exploration of Paul's spirituality, we have drawn attention to many significant dimensions of Paul's spirituality. Among these aspects, four foundational pillars or convictions have emerged that hold significance for us today in the twenty-first century:

- The cross and the resurrection of Christ (a new creation);
- the transforming power of grace;
- the gift of faith and the response of good works; and
- the community of believers as the Body of Christ.

This chapter reflects briefly upon these four foundational pillars of Paul's spirituality insofar as they hold importance for our spirituality today. In discussing their significance, this chapter illustrates by way of example how the lives of individual Christians (especially in the more recent past) have lived out these aspects of Paul's spirituality. Their lives are the best witness to the enduring significance of Paul's spirituality for today. Pope Benedict XVI endorsed this approach when he called on Christians to turn to the lives of the saints in order to discover the spirituality of the Scriptures:

> Truly, dear friends, the saints are the best interpreters of the Bible. As they incarnate the word of God in their own lives, they make it more captivating than ever, so that it really speaks to us.[2]

First Foundational Pillar
The Cross and Resurrection of Christ:
A New Creation in Christ

Without doubt the central focus of Paul's spirituality is on the cross and the resurrection. Paul's encounter with the risen Christ transformed his life and helped him see the cross of Christ with new eyes. Paul's starting point was not an intellectual examination, but rather a personal encounter (Acts 9:1-19). The same is true with us as Christians. Our entry into the Christian life begins with baptism when we first encounter the risen Christ and the power of God transforming our lives. When we are baptized, we become a new creation in Christ. Our awareness of who we are, our identity as a new creation in Christ, comes about gradually as we grow into a deeper relationship with Christ within us.

When we are born into the human family, we are also born into a situation where our human nature is fragmented. As Christians we identify this situation as being born in original sin. The consequences of our first parents' rejection of God infected the human race like a virus. Since God created our human nature, it is good and continues to be good. However, human nature has been tarnished or wounded by the virus of sin. As Paul reminds us, on our own we are not able to overcome this weakness of human nature and to do the good that we know we should do. The grace of God that comes to us in baptism is a gift, transforming us into a new creation in Christ and empowering us to overcome our evil inclinations to sin. The effects of the resurrection of Christ are experienced in baptism, where we are empowered with the gift of the Spirit.

On the cross, Christ showed us that he has overcome all evil. Relying on his power, we are able to overcome the tentacles of evil that tend to ensnare us. Not only are we personally empowered to overcome evil in our own lives, but as Christians we also have the mission to work in the manner of Christ toward overcoming evil in our world. Through the power of the Spirit we strive to transform the world using our talents and abilities.

Our spirituality acknowledges that we are God's children by adoption in the Spirit. "God sent his Son, born of a woman, born under the law, to ransom those under the law, so that we might receive adoption. As proof that you are children, God sent the spirit of his Son into our hearts, crying out, 'Abba, Father!' So you are no longer a slave but a child, and if a child then also an heir, through God" (Gal 4:4-7; see also Gal 3:26; Rom 8:15; 9:26). We have all been made God's adopted children through the expiating death of Jesus on the cross. One's identity as a child of God is connected to and dependent upon one's relationship with God and Jesus Christ, and with all others who are God's children. There can be no discrimination or rejection of others in the community of the children of God, as Paul says, "There is neither Jew nor Greek, there is neither slave nor free person, there is not male and female; for you are all one in Christ Jesus" (Gal 3:28). In Christ all distinctions among people disappear. We are all one in Christ Jesus.

Through the power of the Spirit communicated to us, we are now able to lead a truly spiritual life, a life in which we share in Christ's death and resurrection and are in relationship with the God who is Father, Son, and Spirit. Paul lived out his relationship with God in everything he did. "Moreover, why are we endangering ourselves all the time? Every day I face death" (1 Cor 15:30-31). Paul shows a unique way of leading life: without any form of anxiety. I know that God is with me, that I have been transformed by God's grace; that I am a child of God. Christ is with me, he is in me. There is nothing I should fear. Furthermore, my belief in the resurrection also means I believe that there is a purpose to my life, that there is a future life with God for all eternity. Seen in this context, all fears should dissipate. Our lives take on a totally different perspective.

Christ's death on the cross is not a justification for suffering. Rather it is an identification with all those who do suffer in our world. Suffering is part of the reality of human existence. It is not something God intends. Suffering is a consequence of humanity's ability to choose evil. Christ's death on the cross is no masochistic embrace of suffering; neither is it an acknowledgement that we should seek out suffering for its own sake. By embracing suffering on the cross, Christ has shown us that he is willing to identify with those who suffer and that suffering and death are not ends in themselves. Beyond suffering and death lie the transformation and the resurrection. In the midst of suffering there is always hope. In a concrete way this speaks to our own spirituality today. There are so many situations in which people find themselves where they are helpless and victims of the power that others hold over them. Our response to such situations is not simply to accept them as part of God's plan. God never endorses abuse situations. He demands us to call out situations like these where people are helpless and feel they have no escape. At the same time, if one is in such a situation oneself, it is significant that one does everything to free oneself. Unfortunately, sometimes

Christians think they must accept such situations of suffering. Nothing could be further from the truth. We must always strive to liberate ourselves and others from the powers that dominate our lives.

Nancy Duff gives a remarkable example of this need to extract ourselves from such situations of abuse of power:

> [T]he logic of the cross is not that we are able to become victims consistent with Christ hanging on the cross, but that Christ became a victim to release us from the powers of sin and death. The abused wife does not "represent Christ" through exemplary self-sacrificial love. She is not the incarnate God suffering on behalf of sinful humanity. Rather, Christ on the cross represents her, reveals God's presence with her, and uncovers the sin of those who abuse or neglect her. Christ makes known to her and the world that her suffering represents the *opposite* of God's will.[3]

Paul shows us a further insight into the significance of the death and resurrection of Jesus Christ. In Philippians 2:6-11, the hymn about the humiliation and exaltation of Jesus Christ that we have quoted frequently, Paul proclaims that God has exalted his Son from the humiliation of death to become Lord of the universe:

> [T]hat at the name of Jesus
> every knee should bend,
> of those in heaven and on earth and under the earth,
> and every tongue confess that
> Jesus Christ is Lord,
> to the glory of God the Father. (2:10-11)

This confession proclaims that our spirituality is guided by the belief that there is no area in human life that is not under the Lordship, the rule, of the crucified and risen Jesus. Jesus Christ has shown how we are to be human: the essence is to be self-giving, not self-centered. Most importantly, it demands we acknowledge the positon Jesus Christ holds in our lives. Our allegiance is first and foremost to him as Lord of the universe. In our world today, so many obstacles lie in our path that can undermine our allegiance to Christ as the center of our universe. As we reflect on our own spirituality, the challenge that our belief in Jesus Christ as Lord poses to us is this: "What forces tend to control our lives? Wealth, sex, drugs, power?" In themselves they are all good as part of God's creation. But the problem emerges when they replace the power of Christ in our lives, especially when we succumb to addictions, where these forces enslave us and the rule of Christ in our lives is replaced by the rule of money, sex, drugs, power over another, etc. In this sense, Paul's spirituality is as vital for our world today as it was for his own world.

St. Kateri Tekakwitha (1656–1680)

A Cruciform Spirituality

> Kateri [Tekakwitha] impresses us by the action of grace in her life in spite of the absence of external help and by the courage of her vocation, so unusual in her culture. In her, faith and culture enrich each other! May her example help us to live where we are, loving Jesus without denying who we are! Saint Kateri, Protectress of Canada and the first native American saint, we entrust to you the renewal of the faith in the first nations and in all of North America! May God bless the first nations![4]

The above words come from Pope Benedict XVI's homily on October 21, 2012, at the canonization ceremony of St. Kateri Tekakwitha in Rome. She is the first Native American to be canonized. I refer to her to illustrate an aspect of Paul's spirituality that shows the power the cross of Christ had in her faith and in her life. Hers is truly a "Cruciform Spirituality."

Born more than 300 years ago in a Mohawk village, Ossernion (called today Asierville, forty miles from Albany, NY), she was named Tekakwitha at birth. She would be given the baptismal name, Kateri, later when she was twenty years of age. Her mother, a Christian Algonquin woman, was captured in a raid by the Iroquois and given as wife to the chief of the Mohawk clan (the strongest of the Five Nations League). This was a time of great turmoil in the eastern part of North America: fierce fighting was occurring between the various Native American tribes; North America was being colonized; deadly diseases were spreading among the Native American populations. This was also the area and the time when French Jesuit priests preached and endeavored to spread Christianity among the native populations.

Kateri was four years old when her parents and younger brother died in a smallpox epidemic. She also contracted the disease, but survived. Disfigured with permanent scars on her face, she was left partially blind. She was brought up by an aunt and an uncle, who succeeded her father as chief. Her uncle hated the presence of the Blackrobes (the Jesuit missionaries), but there was nothing he could do since the Iroquois had entered into a treaty with the French that required them to be admitted into villages where there were Christian captives.

Kateri was intrigued by the words of three Blackrobes who were present in her village, but from fear of her uncle she hesitated converting. After refusing to marry a Mohawk man, she was baptized on Easter Sunday at the age of twenty and given the baptismal name Kateri, after St. Catherine of Sienna, her patron Saint. (Kateri is a derivation from the French name for Catherine.) Her conversion made life more difficult for her because of the hostility of her uncle and the tribe toward Christianity. In many ways she had always been an outsider. Her eyesight caused her to avoid direct sunlight so she did not mix outdoors with other girls her age; she also tried to cover her scarred face by wearing a blanket over her head. Now, by becoming a Catholic, she was further ostracized. She was ridiculed even by children for her Christian faith.

Following the advice of a priest, she decided to leave her village for one where she would be supported in her faith. She ran away one night and journeyed to the Christian village of Sault St. Louis that is near present-day Montreal in Canada on the banks of the St. Lawrence River.

Here Kateri grew in her faith and under the spiritual guidance of a Jesuit priest and an older Iroquois woman, Anastasia, who had been a friend of her mother. Kateri loved to find peace and solitude where she could pray, often outdoors and close to nature. Daily Mass was central to her life. She willingly imposed upon herself many rather severe penances. She is said to have walked barefoot in the snow, prayed for hours in the chapel on her knees, and slept on the floor on a bed of thorns. To people today these self-inflicted penances may appear strange, cruel, and unhealthy. However, one should realize that this was part of the spirituality of the time: an ascetic spirituality that attempted to avoid any form of temptation and to keep one's body under control. Kateri undertook fasting as penance on behalf of her nation. Many people say that the punishments she inflicted on her body probably contributed to her early death at the age of twenty-four.

After her arrival in Montreal, Kateri made her First Holy Communion. Her faith grew stronger, and after three years, at the age of twenty-three, she took a vow of virginity. Without doubt this was a stunning decision to make for a Mohawk woman. Given the context of the time, a woman's survival within that society required a husband to provide for her and children to carry on their lineage and to support her in old age.

She died prematurely at the age of twenty-four on the afternoon before Holy Thursday, 1680. Shortly after her death, witnesses claimed that her face changed to look like that of a healthy child and her pockmarks disappeared. The petition for her canonization was made in 1884. She was declared blessed by Pope John Paul II in 1980 and was canonized on October 21, 2012, by Pope Benedict XVI.

St. Kateri's Spirituality for Today

One of the most striking features in Kateri's spiritual life is the evident working of the transforming power of God's grace. Even though her mother died when she was four years old, it was as though her mother had been able to pass onto her a desire for the Catholic faith from birth. God's grace always works in surprising ways, as we have seen in the life of Paul and in the lives of so many saints throughout the centuries. Despite being rejected and ostracized by her own people, like Jesus and Paul, Kateri continued to pursue her yearning for the faith. Her firm commitment to her newfound faith brought her strength, peace, and joy. Kateri witnessed to her allegiance and commitment to the Lordship of Jesus Christ over everything else in her life.

Because of this rejection, she sought support in another Native American community where her faith was ultimately able to grow and flourish. One might imagine her as similar to so many of the converts that Paul brought into his Christian communities. Often when they made the decision to follow Christ, they were not joined by their own families and found themselves ostracized as well.

The Jesuit missionaries in French Canada and in the northern parts of the United States are in many ways like the missionary Paul. They moved from place to place setting up Catholic communities and bringing the message of the Gospel to the peoples of the new world. Without doubt the reality of the cross was at the heart of Kateri's spiritual life. She identified herself with the struggles and sufferings of the crucified Christ.

Kateri exemplifies a cruciform spirituality in her acceptance of suffering. While such extreme forms of penances may appear to be shocking and unhealthy to our modern-day sensitivities, through them, Kateri teaches us that suffering is part of the mystery of life. The life, death, and resurrection of Jesus teach us the positive role of suffering in life. Through Jesus' death on the cross, salvation came to humanity. In like manner, Kateri offered her life and her suffering on behalf of her own people for their salvation. She discovered and entered into the mystery of suffering. Through suffering, Kateri experienced the ultimate transformation and resurrection into the fullness of life with God. Her whole life, as noted, was one of suffering that began in childhood with the scars on her face, her limited eyesight, and her own physical health. All these she accepted because of her identification with Christ and her desire to bear these sufferings on behalf of her nation.

For the modern world today, Kateri teaches that one is to embrace one's situation in life. So often people complain about the difficulties of their lives; they look on themselves as victims and cannot see beyond where they are. Kateri adopted a totally different vision on the world. She embraced her situation with an openness to God's grace working out her salvation. She shows us what so many saints throughout the centuries have demonstrated: faith flourishes in the midst of the cross. The cross is to be embraced, not shunned. The hallmarks of Christian piety throughout the centuries, going back to the people of Israel and handed onto us by Jesus in his Sermon on the Mount, are evident in Kateri's life as well: prayer, fasting, and almsgiving (see Matt 6:1-18).

Second Foundational Pillar
The Transforming Power of Grace

All Is Grace

One of the most significant spiritual lessons one can take from Paul's writings is that all is grace. There are two sides to Paul's consideration of grace. On the one hand, God is the source and origin of every blessing, of every grace. On the other hand, the believer is the recipient of God's blessings and grace. God's grace is transformative and empowering. Grace transforms the human person through the power of the Spirit and the sacraments into a new creation in Christ. Grace also empowers believers to live faithfully as Christ's followers and to accomplish the plan the Lord has for them.

The death and resurrection of Jesus is the foundation for one's understanding of the concept of God's grace. Paul's spirituality demonstrates a firm belief that Christ's death on the cross is the greatest illustration of God's love for humanity. Paul does not place his emphasis on the death of Jesus as the result of a vindictive God who is punishing his Son for our sins. Instead, Paul's spirituality always views God as a loving God who is deeply concerned for humanity. Jesus accepted his death on the cross voluntarily as an atonement for our sins, as Paul says in his famous hymn, "he humbled himself, / becoming obedient to death, / even death on a cross" (Phil 2:8). William Placher expresses well the concern Paul has in talking about the death of Jesus for our sins, "he actively accepts suffering for the sake of transforming the world."[5]

Later Christian theologians reflected endlessly on the question of how this atonement takes place. Numerous theories have been proposed to explain how Christ substituted himself for us on the cross. However, this is not where Paul's spirituality is focused. Paul is more concerned about illustrating or drawing out the reasons why Christ died on the cross. For Paul, Christ's death was the way in which God demonstrated how much God loved humanity. Christ's death shows the extent to which Christ went by identifying himself with us in death. There is no limitation to God's love for us. God's love is unconditional. This unconditional love is expressed for enemies and for sinners. Love is transformative in that it has the power to transform the lives of enemies into friends. Paul's experience of the risen Christ is the clearest evidence of this transformative power of God's love. Paul was an enemy of the cross, but his encounter with the risen Christ transformed his spiritual life to become Christ's greatest advocate. Having experienced Christ's love for him, Paul responded by reaching out to others to share this love for them.

God Identifies with Those Who Suffer

The entire Scriptures (Old and New Testament) present the image of a God who champions the cause of the oppressed. In the life and ministry of God's Son, God goes further than simply championing the cause of those who suffer. God identifies with them through his Son's death. The cross is not an end in itself; instead, it is the passageway to the resurrection. The cross-resurrection paradigm shows that in the midst of suffering, God is there with his grace as the seed of transformation. The negativity and evil of the cross is transformed into the glory of the resurrected life. In this sense, through the paradigm of the cross-resurrection, those who suffer are given the grace to persevere as well as the pledge that they will ultimately experience the transformation of victory over their suffering. Just as Christ's suffering was freely accepted, it benefited not only Christ himself but all humanity. This offers a further paradigm for those who suffer. In imitation of Christ, they are challenged to embrace their suffering as Christ did for the benefit of others.

As argued previously, the acceptance of suffering is in no way intended to be masochistic, nor is it intended to oppress the weak and the powerless by those who are powerful: this would in fact be an abuse of the cross. The value of suffering on behalf of others is without doubt a central vision of Paul's spirituality as he reflects upon the significance of the cross-resurrection. There are serious implications that need to be drawn from this insight into the acceptance and freely chosen suffering on behalf of others. This spiritual vision is at odds with what has come to be known today in many Christian circles as "the prosperity gospel." Such a spirituality promises success, financial rewards, and the avoidance of all struggles and suffering, provided that one contributes financially to certain church-sponsored causes. This is a modern form of Greek paganism whereby one buys the favor of the gods by his or her gifts to them. By giving money in this way, one is being promised a guarantee of financial rewards (*quid pro quo*). Without doubt this is a distortion of the Christian message and paradigm of the cross-resurrection. Paul's spirituality never promised his followers a life of ease. Luke Timothy Johnson emphasizes this point when he writes that, at its core, the spirituality of Christian discipleship must embrace suffering and service in imitation of Christ Jesus:

> The imitation of Christ in his life of suffering and service—not as an act of masochism for the sake of suppressing one's own life but as an act of love for the enhancement of others' life—is not an optional version of Christian identity. It is the very *essence* of Christian identity. It is the pattern by which every other claim about the spiritual life must be measured if it is to be considered Christian. It is what is learned from Jesus. It is what learning Jesus means.[6]

Father Stanley Rother (1935–1981)

Missionary and Martyr

Seldom do we hear of modern-day United States missionaries and martyrs. Yet there are many.[7] Father Stanley Rother was one such missionary and martyr. He worked for more than thirteen years as a missionary among the Tzutujil Mayans on the shores of Lake Santiago Atitlán in Guatemala before his assassination on July 28, 1981.

Stan Rother was an ordinary young man whose dedication to God and his people was remarkable. In a sense, his dedication was like that of St. Paul centuries before. Stan was born in 1935 and grew up on a farm in Oklahoma. He studied for the priesthood for the Archdiocese of Oklahoma City. His first attempt to study for the priesthood was unsuccessful largely because his greatest obstacle was learning Latin (a difficulty many young men encountered in those years prior to the Second Vatican Council [1962–1965]). On his second attempt, supported by an understanding Bishop Victor Reed, Stan completed his seminary training and was ordained on May 25, 1963.[8]

In 1968, after five years as a priest, Fr. Stan Rother volunteered to go to a mission in Guatemala. Stan immersed himself in the mission. He set out to serve his people both spiritually and materially. Spiritually, he visited the homes of the people; he said five Masses in different places each Sunday and baptized in the range of one thousand people a year. Like Paul who worked as a tent maker, Stan worked at rebuilding the church, erecting a clinic, and raising crops on a farm that belonged to the parish. These were just some of the physical labors that endeared him to his people. Growing up on a farm, he was able to teach the local people methods of farming and many skills suited to their agricultural environment. He learned their language and they called him Padre Aplas.

In 1980 the civil war that had been raging in Guatemala reached the area where Stan was working. A number of people whom Stan knew well as part of his parish were executed by the death squads. Stan tried hard to stay out of the political struggles that were raging around him. But he could not stop reaching out to those whom the army had marked for execution and their families. One notable incident occurred when a group of guerrillas attacked the army and in retaliation the army executed seventeen innocent civilians in the area around Santiago Atitlán. Stan had the bodies brought into his church for burial. Probably actions like these aroused the animosity of the army against him.

In January 1981, Stan was warned that his name had appeared on a death list and was urged to return to the United States as his life was in danger. Reluctantly, he returned to his family home, the farm where he grew up. He spent three months there and helped out in local parishes giving many talks about the situation in Guatemala. But he realized he needed to return to his people.

Archbishop John Quinn, a former Archbishop of Oklahoma City, describes well his decision to return:

> But he just couldn't stay away. He told his parents, "The shepherd can't run away. I have to go back." And so knowing that he was facing certain death, he returned to his people. But the Holy Spirit, who reminds us and makes plain all that Jesus has said, deepened in Stan Rother the understanding that "the good shepherd lays down his life for his sheep."[9]

In May 1981, he returned to his parish mission in Santiago Atitlán to be with his people to celebrate Holy Week with them.[10] Three months later on July 28, 1981, three masked men broke into his bedroom in the rectory and shot him twice (one shot was fired with a gun pressed against his temple). Stan had told friends that he was not going to let himself be taken away to be tortured. He put up a fight. A bullet found at the scene was identified as one used in a Smith and Wesson, the type used by the army. No one has ever been convicted for Stan's death.

Stan's body was brought back to Oklahoma where it was buried. His heart, according to the burial practices of the Tzutujil Mayans, was removed and enshrined in the church in Santiago Atitlán. Over three thousand people attended Fr. Stan's funeral. His cause for canonization has been filed in Rome by the Archdiocese of Oklahoma.

Father Stan Rother's Spirituality for Today

Many aspects of the life and death of Fr. Stan Rother mirror St. Paul's life and spirituality. Like Paul, Stan was a missionary who brought the gospel message far from his own home to people who were considered outcasts in the world. He went from the comfort and security of life in the United States to the hardships of a third-world country. Struggles and difficulties were part of his life's work. Like Paul, a tent maker, Stan relied upon his own industrious hard work to support himself and the people of his parish. Like Paul, who returned to Jerusalem on his third missionary journey with the knowledge that he would be arrested, so Stan returned to Guatemala knowing that he would face death. Paul rejoiced in the sufferings and hardships he endured because he saw them all as sharing in the sufferings of Christ. Stan also viewed the life of Jesus as his model, "A good shepherd lays down his life for the sheep" (John 10:11). He did not return to Guatemala because he considered it an obligation. Rather, he followed the inspiration and example of Jesus. He identified his life with that of Christ. Out of love for the people whom he served, Stan returned and ultimately gave his life for his people.

We see the transforming power of God's grace throughout Stan's life. From the beginning, God was preparing him for his task in life. Growing up on a farm and learning what was necessary for sustaining life, Stan was able to use these gifts and share them with others in his mission church. The obstacles he faced in the seminary were surely overcome by God's grace. His spirituality ignited him to serve his people both spiritually and physically and help them experience God's love through his own life and example. Finally, the desire to return to his own people in Guatemala, despite the knowledge that he may face death, could be undertaken only through the strength and power of God's Spirit and grace guiding him.

While most will never face the possibility of dying as a martyr for their faith, people learn through the life and spirituality of Fr. Stan Rother that they can remain true only to their vocation in life if they are open to God's Spirit guiding them. From the dedication and love that he showed the people he served, he is an example and inspiration to each of us in our life's journey. His inspiration lies especially in being a witness to God's transforming grace working in his life. We all face struggles and difficulties in life. There are times when we feel overwhelmed and perhaps want to throw it all away. In instances like these, Fr. Stan reminds us that it is only through the strength and power of God's grace that we can remain true to our calling and persevere along that path. Despite his faith and his life being challenged, he was able to remain true to his convictions and belief. Only God's grace could give him the strength needed to return to Guatemala and face the strong possibility that he would be killed. His fidelity and strength inspire one to face one's daily challenges with a similar trust in the power of God's grace working and transforming one's life.

Third Foundational Pillar
The Gift of Faith Responds in Good Works of Love

The legacy of Paul's spirituality is rich and varied. Perhaps most significantly, his spirituality is one that is always open to change, to growth, and to development. Previously, he had believed that he maintained his relationship with God through fidelity to works of the law. Then he saw his relationship with God through Christ as coming through the grace of faith.

Like Paul, our spirituality must remain open to change and growth as we are guided by the Holy Spirit in our lives. The Spirit brought Paul to the realization that his former spirituality, driven by a focus on works of the law, was inadequate and could never lead to fidelity to God's covenantal relationship. Only a spirituality that is led by the grace of the risen Christ can remain faithful to this covenant relationship. The center of our spirituality must remain our spiritual relationship with Christ in faith (Gal 3:7-13).

Paul's spirituality has shown us that God's love invites us into the covenant relationship established through his Son's death on the cross. Christian spirituality does not begin with laws and rules, but is founded upon and sustained by a relationship with Christ that is both personal and communal. Our identity is shaped by being in Christ, and our faith comes to us through the gift of God's grace. Faith means being united to Christ and living life in love. By living in relationship with Christ, we lead lives as Christ led his, by works of love for others—and we will be judged by our love for others on the last day.

Like Paul, our spirituality must always remain open to the guidance of the Holy Spirit in our lives. A remarkable illustration of this has happened recently among the Lutheran World Federation and the Roman Catholic Church. Openness to the guidance of the Holy Spirit has brought these churches to a common agreement in understanding the relationship between faith and works of love. Reflecting together on the Sacred Scriptures, especially the spirituality of Paul, they have come to a common agreement that moves beyond the disputes of the Reformation era over the doctrine on justification by faith. This agreement reversed centuries of animosity and misunderstanding between the Lutheran World Federation and the Roman Catholic Church:

> We [the Lutheran World Federation and the Roman Catholic Church] confess together that sinners are justified by faith in the saving action of God in Christ. By the action of the Holy Spirit in baptism, they are granted the gift of salvation, which lays the basis for the whole Christian life. They place their trust in God's gracious promise by justifying faith, which includes hope in God and love for him. Such a faith is active in love and thus the Christian cannot and should not remain without works. But whatever in the justified precedes or follows the free gift of faith is neither the basis of justification nor merits it.[11]

Faith Active in Love

The identification of Christ Jesus with us in suffering is a supreme example of God's love for us. As shown throughout this exploration of Paul's spirituality, love for others is at the heart of Paul's spirituality. Love is not to be understood in a romanticized form as sometimes his hymn to love (1 Corinthians 13) is understood. Love, for Paul, is more than just an emotion, it is above all an empathy for the other, being able to walk in another's shoes. Love enables us to see others through the eyes of God, through the power of God's Spirit. The origin of love resides in God; it is a grace. This gift of love begins with God and enables one to respond to God and to others with the same love (2 Cor 5:14-19).

The power of Christ's love in us energizes our own spirituality enabling us to view everyone differently. We think about others from a totally different perspective. "Whoever is in Christ is a new creation!" Those in

Christ have been transformed just as we have been transformed. For this very reason we treat everyone differently. We are controlled by Christ's love and allow that love to work in and through us. In the confines of our own world we spread the transforming power of God's love to others.

Love is always other-centered. This love is countercultural and challenges our modern world that is driven by individualism and self-centeredness. The death of Jesus on the cross teaches that a true spirituality cannot be individualist and isolationist but must always be empowered by a desire to serve others, to act in love for others. Paul's spirituality has also shown that a remarkable consequence of living life for others is the spirit of joy and peace. Joy is certainly one of the fruits of the Holy Spirit and is a wonderful illustration of the serenity that comes from living for others.

A further dimension of a spirituality that makes faith alive in love is the realization that one strives to bring the love of Christ to others. The questions one needs to pose oneself are, among others: "How can the love of Christ speak to the context of a particular person or group?" "How can that love be made incarnate in a certain situation or time?" These are questions that above all demonstrate an awareness and sensitivity to the other.

Finally, a spirituality that embraces love in action brings love into situations where people have lost hope, shows people that no matter how difficult and hopeless a situation may be, God's love is present there. Paul reminds us that there is nothing that can separate us from the love of God in Christ Jesus. He asks the rhetorical question: "What will separate us from the love of Christ? Will anguish, or distress, or persecution, or famine, or nakedness, or peril, or the sword?" He answers his own question by saying, "No, in all things we conquer overwhelmingly through him who loved us" (Rom 8:35-37). Ours is the task to help people experience Christ's love in these situations. The crucifix is a wonderful symbol that reminds people of the cost of God's love for humanity. At the same time the crucifix always points beyond itself to the hope of the resurrection.

Mother Antonia Brenner (1926–2013)

"The Prison Angel"

"Sister Antonia Brenner dies at 86; nun moved into Tijuana prison to tend to inmates": Such was the headline in the *Los Angeles Times* that first introduced me to the life of a remarkable woman who touched the lives of thousands in such an extraordinary yet ordinary way.[12] The more one learns about her life story and her outreach of love and service, the more one sees reflected Paul's spirituality that the gift of true faith responds in works of love. The life of Mother Antonia (*La Madre Antonia*, or simply *La Mama*, as she was always called in the Mexican Prison of La Mesa in Tijuana, Mexico, by prisoners and guards alike) shows us the essence of faith. Faith is alive, it is passionate. Faith is living life in service of others. Faith brings Christ's love to everyone, especially those most rejected by society. There is no better way to express Paul's understanding of faith than by looking briefly at the life of this courageous and inspiring woman.

Mother Antonia was born Mary Clarke in Los Angeles on December 1, 1926. Later her family moved to Beverly Hills, where they were neighbors of some of the great movie stars of those days. Her father, Joseph (a first-generation Irish-American), had grown up in New York from a very poor, humble background, and, after many setbacks, had become a successful businessman. Despite his success and his wealth, he set a great example to his children in living a life of simplicity and of helping the poor. For example, instead of taking the streetcar, he used to walk to work. The money he saved was given to Maryknoll Missionaries.[13]

Mary's first marriage at the age of nineteen did not work out. She remarried shortly afterward, but again this marriage would end in divorce. Mary raised four daughters and three sons, experiencing the same struggles and difficulties of all single mothers in raising seven children. At the same time, she became increasingly involved in charity work. A priest from Pasadena, California, invited Mary to join him on a trip to Tijuana, Mexico, to deliver medicines, food, and clothing to the poor. They visited La Mesa, an infamous state penitentiary in Tijuana known for its violence, drugs, corruption, and death, and delivered supplies to the prison infirmary. That chance visit changed the direction of her life. She continued to visit the prison and each visit was a source of inspiration that filled her with compassion. She would drive truckloads of supplies to the prison over the course of the following years and spend more and more time visiting the prison.

On March 19, 1977, after much soul-searching, Mary made an important decision. Most of her family were now grown up. She sold her home and set out to work full time in the penitentiary of La Mesa to serve the prisoners there. She was not able to join a religious community as she had been divorced and, being fifty years of age, she was considered too old. This did not stop her dedication to what she knew the Lord wanted her to do. She took private vows, donned a religious habit, and chose the name Mother Antonia in order to serve the inmates of La Mesa Penitentiary.[14] The remaining thirty-six years of her life were dedicated to caring for the needs of the prisoners and the guards, as well as their family members outside the prison. Seeing the significant and dedicated work she was doing, the bishops of Tijuana and San Diego supported her ministry wholeheartedly.

Mother Antonia lived in the prison just as all the other prisoners did. She was given a cell, ten feet by ten feet, ate the same food, and showered in cold water as the prisoners did. She mixed with the inmates, helping them in whatever way she could. She gave comfort to them when loved ones on the outside passed away. She witnessed prisoners kill one another and die from illness. She buried those who had no relatives to claim their bodies. In her cell she kept supplies for the prisoners, such as toilet paper. There's a fascinating story told of how she went to a grocery store in San Diego and asked the owner if he would donate a case of toilet paper. The owner was surprised by such a request and asked her why she wanted so much. She told him she needed it for prisoners at La Mesa and then she added, "Have you ever gone to the bathroom and tried to clean yourself when you don't have any toilet paper? How would you feel?"[15] This grocery store owner became one of her many supporters and suppliers of goods.

One story stands out in her ministry at La Mesa and illustrates how the inmates accepted her and how God's love touched their lives through her. On Halloween night, 1994, a riot broke out with the inmates taking over the prison. Mother Antonia intervened, unconcerned about her own life and safety. She was alone in the prison, in the dark, with prisoners:

> She can feel the heavy black metal doors of cells as she passes them. The screams and shooting are close now, the smoke is sharp in her eyes and lungs. She calls out to the men in the punishment cells.
> They are shocked to hear her.
> "Don't shoot! Mother's here!" they yell.
> "Mother Antonia! Get out of here. You'll be killed!" one inmate shouts, "Please go. You'll be shot!"
> She doesn't stop. She moves forward toward their voices.
> "What's going on here? The whole city is terrified," she says. "Your mothers and girlfriends and children are outside crying. Please stop. There's an army out there getting ready to come in."
> She tells them that if they don't put down their weapons, more children will be orphaned, including their own. Think of your parents crying at another family funeral, she pleads. Her voice is warm, convincing, and it suddenly changes the ugly night.[16]

The inmates listened to her. She mediated on their behalf with the prison authorities. A settlement was reached: the prisoners ended the riot, the authorities promised to address the concerns of the prisoners. Mother Antonia had resolved peacefully a situation that could have ended in bloodshed with many lives lost.

La Mesa continued to receive support and help as people learned of Mother Antonia's dedication. The bishops of Tijuana and San Diego encouraged her to found a religious community of women like herself who were in their later years of life, rich in their own life experiences. Her community was called the "Eudist Servants of the Eleventh Hour." "The Eleventh Hour" refers to those who join the community and are late in life (between forty-five and sixty-five years of age). "Eudist" identifies them as a part of the international Eudist family named after St. John Eudes (1601–1680) who founded the Congregation of Jesus and Mary (CJM). Over the centuries, other branches were incorporated into this family. Mother Antonia's community was formally recognized by the bishop of Tijuana in 2003. Her religious community has a house in Tijuana itself. Families of prisoners who have nowhere to stay when they come to visit their family members at La Mesa are accommodated in the sisters' house.

During the thirty-six years working and living in La Mesa, Mother Antonia remained in contact with her children and grandchildren who often visited her. Her work drew praise from President Reagan of the United States and President Fox of Mexico. Being a person of energy and action, she did not write much. Her words that have survived are those she spoke in interviews, talks, and more especially in personal conversations that have touched and changed the lives of thousands of people. Mother Antonia passed away on October 17, 2013, at the age of eighty-six in Tijuana.

Mother Antonia's Spirituality for Today

Mother Antonia's life and spirituality show so well how God's grace transformed and sustained her throughout her life. Many aspects of her life resemble those of St. Paul. Like his, her life experienced a total transformation. A chance visit to La Mesa in Tijuana gave her a new passion for helping others and energized her faith for thirty-six years. After a number of visits to La Mesa, she had a dream that shows so clearly how her faith was inspired by Christ:

> One night in 1969 she had a dream so vivid that she shot out of bed to write it down. She was a prisoner about to be executed, and Christ came to take her place. She was sure the dream was about La Mesa and how she should be coming to the aid of the most desper-

ate prisoners. That dream reinforced her sense that she was meant to be at La Mesa, where she had come to feel at home. She felt most like herself when she was there, more energized and more vital.[17]

Passion lies at the heart of every spirituality, an energy that gives direction to life. The lives of both Paul and Mother Antonia were guided and directed by their faith experiences of the risen Christ, albeit in different ways. Paul's spirituality showed that faith needs to be expressed in works of love. This was the heart of his spiritual message. As Paul says in his well-known hymn in 1 Corinthians 13, love is the greatest of all gifts. Mother Antonia's whole life was guided by her love and service of others, especially for those whom society considers unlovable, those who have committed crimes and are imprisoned. Mother Antonia's life work was to show that those who commit crimes and those who are victims of crime are human beings like ourselves. Everyone needs to be treated with love and respect. Those in prison also have family members who suffer as a result of their situation. Mother Antonia never condoned the crimes that were committed. She always challenged the prisoners to admit their crimes and seek forgiveness from God and those they had hurt. At the same time, she cared for them in every way she could. She looked after the families outside the prison and endeavored to make life tolerable for all. Her works of love clearly illustrate Jesus' message in his final parable, the Judgment of the Nations, "For I was hungry and you gave me food, I was thirsty and you gave me drink, a stranger and you welcomed me, naked and you clothed me, ill and you cared for me, in prison and you visited me . . . Amen, I say to you, whatever you did for one of these least brothers of mine, you did for me" (Matt 25:35-36, 40). Mother Antonia's faith energized her to serve "these least brothers and sisters of mine."

Mother Antonia's spirituality should inspire each one of us to reach out in love and compassion for the most unfortunate members of our society, especially for those others considered unlovable. While one may not be called to serve the needs of those imprisoned (though some surely are), there are so many other areas where faith in the risen Christ calls one to action: helping those who are homebound or sick, caring for those who are lonely, or simply being a listener for someone who has no one else to talk to. All these are people in need.

A Spirituality for Our Later Years: The unique example that Mother Antonia sets for all of us is to show that at every stage of life we need to rediscover our passion for life and for service of others. Even in our later years of life, Christ is calling us to use our life experiences in the service of others. So often when we grow older, when we retire, we feel that we still have much to offer. Mother Antonia shows us that in those years, when we have time at our disposal, we can discover a new passion in life for helping others. Without doubt she shows us a secret discovery in helping others: we are touched, we are transformed, just as much as are those whom we are helping.

A Spirituality Guided by Conviction: A further dimension of Mother Antonia's spirituality that illustrates Paul's life and has a great significance for our own spirituality is Paul's conviction that "'My grace is sufficient for you, for power is made perfect in weakness' . . . Therefore, I am content with weaknesses, insults, hardships, persecutions, and constraints, for the sake of Christ; for when I am weak, then I am strong" (2 Cor 12:9-10). Mother Antonia demonstrated that it was the power of Christ that enabled her to do so many things despite her age and her health. Her spirituality challenges us to see in life's challenges a way to turn to Christ and draw strength from the promise made through Paul. Truly when we are weak, when we feel that we do not have the strength to carry on, that is the time that the risen Christ is close to us to empower us with his grace to accomplish what on our own we are unable to do.

Finally, joy and happiness are key virtues emanating from Mother Antonia's life. Paul's life was also one that was characterized by the spirit of joy. His letter to the Philippians exudes joy—joy, even though he is in prison, not knowing what the outcome will be. The joy of the Holy Spirit comes through the strength God gives us. Joy comes from the power of our faith in the risen Christ. The same is true of Mother Antonia. In an interview she gave to the Washington Post in 2002, she spoke about happiness:

> Pleasure depends on where you are, who you are with, what you are eating. Happiness is different. *Happiness* does not depend on where you are. I live in prison. And I have not had a day of depression in 25 years. I have been upset, angry. I have been sad. But never depressed. I have a reason for my being.[18]

Happiness does not depend on where you are or on what you have. Some of the happiest people I have witnessed are in the poorest villages in Africa where children play with plastic bags rolled up to make a soccer ball or people gather together in the evenings around a fire with someone beating a homemade drum fashioned out of discarded tins and animal skins. Joy and happiness come from living with others and for others. How different from our consumer-oriented society that thinks happiness is derived from the latest gadgets available on the market!

Faith responding in works of love captures the essence of Mother Antonia's spirituality. At every stage of life, the Lord gives us inspiration and strength to share his love with others. All we need is to be open to the inspiration and guidance of the Spirit leading us in surprisingly new directions in love, joy, and happiness.

Fourth Foundational Pillar
The Community of Believers as the Body of Christ

Christian spirituality is always oriented and experienced within the context of a community. Paul's spirituality illustrates this in a number of fundamental ways.

"Put on Christ": In Romans 13:12-14, Paul uses a beautiful image of putting on a garment to capture what Christian spirituality is all about. Just as we take off a dirty garment and put on a clean one, so we turn away from our former way of life and become a totally new creation in Christ. The very life of Christ embraces us and transforms us to live the life of Christ, a life that experiences, as Christ himself did, the cross and the resurrection. Our spirituality takes this transformation seriously. As a new creation, we think differently, we think with the mind of Christ, we look on the world with the eyes of Christ, and we act in the way in which Christ acts. We are able to do this because of the gift of the life of the Spirit that has been communicated to us. We live the life of Christ in the way in which he lived his life: for others. Paul's spirituality teaches us that true Christian spirituality is one that focuses away from ourselves and looks toward the needs and sufferings of others.

A Spirituality Enlivened by the Sacraments

Paul's spirituality developed through experiencing the worship life of those Christian communities he had founded. Their worship life both created and enlivened those communities. In thinking about Paul's life, we are always reminded of a person who lived for others. From the time of his conversion onward, Paul spent his life spreading Jesus' message and bringing others into relationship with Jesus. Our Christian journey begins when we put on Christ in the sacrament of baptism. In baptism we are brought into a relationship with Christ and with the community as the Body of Christ. We celebrate the Eucharist together with others in community. Whenever we celebrate the Eucharist, we "eat this bread and drink the cup, [and] proclaim the death of the Lord until he comes" (1 Cor 11:26). As the Eucharistic celebration nourishes us and continues to transform our lives, we have the task of living that life as we go from the community to bring the love of Christ to others, to help them to experience the transforming power of his love in their own lives.

The Spirituality of the Body of Christ

This image of the Body of Christ is unique to Paul's spirituality, and, as such, it captures so well its community dimension. As the Body of Christ, each one of us is united to Christ together with others. By this image our spirituality is enlivened by the realization that one has a unique contribution to make to the Body of Christ. The gifts of the Spirit, the abilities and talents that we each possess, have been communicated to each of us for the building up of the Body of Christ. "To each individual the manifestation of the Spirit is given *for some benefit*" (italics added; 1 Cor 12:7). The Spirit unleashes and empowers within one the talents and abilities one has to serve the Body of Christ. As such, each one of us through these gifts makes a special contribution to building up the Body of Christ.

In the Body of Christ, all differences and every form of discrimination come to an end. We are all one in Christ: "There is neither Jew nor Greek, there is neither slave nor free person, there is not male and female; for you are all one in Christ Jesus" (Gal 3:28). Our differences are celebrated and our diversity contributes to the one body of Christ. Christ is the one who transforms this diversity into a unity. Our spirituality calls us to bring all peoples into the Body of Christ. Paul spent his whole life journeying throughout the Roman Empire bringing diverse peoples from different backgrounds, religions, and ethnicities into the one body of Christ. In like manner, with Paul's spirituality as our inspiration, we too welcome all people into this community of the Body of Christ.

Prayer and Community: Prayer is community oriented and sustains the life of the community. Paul's letters abound in prayer for the communities, churches, and individuals who have been part of his journey of life. The opening thanksgiving of the letter to the Philippians illustrates Paul's gratitude to God for the community and church of Philippi in his ministry:

> I give thanks to my God at every remembrance of you, praying always with joy in my every prayer for all of you, because of your part-

nership for the gospel from the first day until now . . . And this is my
prayer: that your love may increase ever more and more in knowledge and every kind of perception. (1:3-4, 9)

Our spirituality as well embraces prayer as the central aspect in uniting ourselves with the lives of others in Christ. We too thank God for the
gift of those in our lives who have contributed to our faith and our love
for God. We unite ourselves in prayer for the needs and sufferings of all
those whom we know as well as all who are part of the Body of Christ.
We pray for God's Spirit to be with them to enable them to accomplish
God's plans, to support them in their struggles and difficulties, and, like
Paul, to thank God for their faith and perseverance.

St. Katharine Drexel (1858–1955)

Missionary and Founder of Communities

St. Katharine Drexel's life and spirituality have had a major influence on the growth and outreach of the Catholic Church in the United
States. Undoubtedly, her lifework among the Native American and African American communities has been largely responsible for propel-
ling the Catholic Church to embrace racial equality and social justice.
She was a century ahead of her time in her dedicated work striving for
civil rights and social justice for all Americans.

Katharine Drexel was born in Philadelphia on November 26, 1858.
Her father, Francis Anthony Drexel, was a business partner of the fi-
nancier J. P. Morgan. Her mother, Hannah Jane (Langstroth), died a
month after Katharine's birth. Two years later, her father remarried to
Emma Bouvier. While her father amassed a great fortune, he used his
wealth in significant philanthropic causes.

Katharine and her younger sister, Louise, were homeschooled by
private tutors. Both parents gave them an inherent love for their faith,
as well as an exposure to the needs of the African American and Native
American communities throughout the country.

Her stepmother died in 1883 and her father in 1885. He left behind a
vast fortune of fifteen-and-a-half million dollars that was to be divided
equally among his three daughters. In order to protect them from those
who might marry them for their money, he structured his will in such a
way that his daughters controlled their income from the estate and on
their deaths their share of the inheritance would pass to their children.
If there were no grandchildren, then on the death of his daughters the
estate would be donated to some designated religious communities
and charities.

After the death of their father, the three daughters went to Europe. In January 1897, they had a private audience with Pope Leo XIII. Katharine spoke to the pope about the needs of the Native American peoples especially for missionary priests in the United States. To her surprise the pope in his turn said to her, "Why not, my child, become yourself a missionary?"[19] Katharine had been considering entering religious life for a number of years, and this was the encouragement she needed. While her spiritual director, Bishop O'Connor of the Nebraska Territories and Omaha, had for a long time discouraged her from entering a convent, he now supported her intention to embrace religious life. Bishop O'Connor went even further and encouraged her to found her own community of sisters in order to work among Native Americans. He wisely realized that should she enter an existing congregation of sisters she might be assigned to some other ministry and would not have the freedom to do what she so desperately wanted to do.

Her decision to enter religious life shocked the wealthy circles of Philadelphia. *The Philadelphia Public Ledger* carried a banner headline: "Miss Drexel Enters a Catholic Convent—Gives up Seven Million."[20] She entrusted her share of the inheritance to the management of her two sisters. She spent twenty months in a convent of the Sisters of Mercy as a postulant and then as a novice where she learned about religious and community life. On February 12, 1891, she took her vows as the founder of a new congregation of sisters, entitled the Sisters of the Blessed Sacrament, dedicated to African American and Native American peoples. Their mission was to work for the care and betterment of those whom they served.

Shortly after making her profession, a motherhouse was constructed in Bensalem, Philadelphia. The day before the blessing of the cornerstone for the new motherhouse, a stick of dynamite was discovered near the site. A neighbor had placed it there showing his strong opposition to a school for black children being built so close to his property. This was the first of many incidents where racial prejudice tried to thwart Mother Katharine and her sisters in their missionary work. She was a pioneer in every conceivable way in working for the education of the Native American and African American peoples. In 1894, she established her first foundation outside the motherhouse, a mission school for Native Americans in Santa Fe, New Mexico. Many other schools were started in the following years. The founding of Xavier University, New Orleans, for African American students in 1915 was probably the most significant of all. "In 1918 the governor of Louisiana signed a bill that allowed Xavier University to award college degrees. The new university grew quickly, and by 1927 had four separate departments, the teacher's college, college of arts and sciences, pre-medicine, and the college of pharmacy."[21]

Throughout her life, Mother Katharine Drexel used the inheritance that came to her for the works of her newly established congregation of sisters as well as to support many other ministries in the wider Catholic Church. At her death in 1955, there were more than five hundred Sisters of the Blessed Sacrament (SBM) in sixty-three schools throughout the United States. She was beatified in November 1988 and canonized on October 1, 2000. She is only the second canonized American-born saint.

Mother Katharine Drexel's Spirituality for Today

A Missionary Spirituality Imbued with Social Justice: There are many areas in her life and faith where Mother Katharine Drexel followed in the footsteps of Paul's spirituality. The clearest illustration was her role as a missionary. Mother Katharine saw that the great need of her time was to reach out with the message of the Gospel for those in our country who were the most neglected and ignored members of society. This was well before the church and society at large showed any concern for the disenfranchised groups within society. Without a doubt Mother Katharine was a pioneer of social justice in the country and in the Catholic Church in the United States. It is fascinating to see that she raised the issue of the situation of Native American peoples with Pope Leo XIII in January 1897, the pope who was himself the pioneer of Catholic Social Teaching with his groundbreaking encyclical, *Rerum Novarum* (or as it is known in English, *The Rights and Duties of Capital and Labor*), issued on May 15, 1891. The Drexel sisters had met the pope in 1887 and one can immediately see that in Pope Leo XII Katharine had discovered that the leader of the Catholic Church was as passionate as she was for the welfare and rights of the powerless in society.

Mother Katharine saw as well the role that education could play in the advancement of the African American and Native American people. Her actions show that the message of Christ embraces all people with dignity, respect, and equality. By striving to incarnate these values of dignity, respect, and equality, the work of Mother Katharine and her sisters has transformed the lives of millions of people over the past century since the foundation of their congregation. This work of transformation truly conforms to Paul's belief that all distinctions among peoples are overcome in the Body of Christ, "There is neither Jew nor Greek, there is neither slave nor free person, there is not male and female; for you are all one in Christ Jesus" (Gal 3:28).

A Kenotic Spirituality: Mother Katharine Drexel's whole life was inspired, directed, and governed by her faith and her spirituality. Cheryl Hughes, in her biography of Drexel, gives a wonderful explanation of Christian Spirituality in general and the type of spirituality that nourished and energized the life and mission of Mother Katharine Drexel. She defines her spirituality as kenotic and eucharistic.[22] *Kenotic* (from the Greek word *kenóō* "to empty") means self-emptying and takes as its inspiration the model of Jesus Christ as outlined in Paul's Letter to the Philippians 2:5-11. Paul begins this hymn with this advice to his readers: "Have among yourselves the same attitude that is also yours in Christ Jesus,

> Who, though he was in the form of God,
> did not regard equality with God something to be grasped.
> Rather, he emptied himself [*heauton ekenōsen*],
> taking the form of a slave.

Without doubt these words capture the life of Mother Katharine. She gave up the life of an heiress and instead embraced a vowed life of poverty. While she did receive the income from her father's estate, she used it exclusively to support her works of social justice. She emulates again Paul's life where he speaks about working as a tent maker so as not to be a burden on his community (Acts 18:1-3). As Paul supported himself by his work, Mother Katharine supported her communities and their works through her inheritance.

A Eucharistic Spirituality Embracing the Body of Christ: In the Eucharist, Mother Katherine experienced Christ's love. Mass and Adoration before the Blessed Sacrament were central to her daily life and spirituality. This love and unity with Christ in the Blessed Sacrament inspired her to name her congregation the "Sisters of the Blessed Sacrament" for the African American and Native American people. The name signifies that Mother Katharine understood that the Eucharist, as the Body of Christ, embraces all people. The love of Christ and our love for Christ in the Eucharist always embraces the love for the whole Body of Christ. This love experienced in the presence of the Blessed Sacrament takes on a missionary dimension in that one has to go out and share that love of Christ with others and experience the presence of Christ in others.

A Spirituality Uniquely Suited to Our Twenty-First Century: As mentioned earlier, Mother Katharine was indeed a century ahead of her time. She showed a concern for social justice issues that are significant in treating every person with dignity, equality, and respect. She used her gifts and talents tirelessly to build up the Body of Christ. Our world today is inspired with the zeal to pursue and uphold social justice in the relationships among all peoples. Mother Katharine is a witness to the power of God's grace working in her life and inspiring the church as the Body of Christ to courageously embrace all peoples and lead them to become part of the Body of Christ. In her openness to the power of God's grace and the guidance of the Holy Spirit, Katharine Drexel witnesses to us and to every generation of the followers of Christ to use the gifts God has given us for the building up of the Body of Christ and for the service of all people. By using our gifts to empower others, we contribute to the transformation of our world where the values of dignity, respect, and equality of all peoples are upheld as sacrosanct within society and within the church. This is undoubtedly the spiritual legacy and spirituality that St. Katharine Drexel has bequeathed to our church, to her congregation, to our society, and especially to each one of us. A legacy and spirituality that continues to be as vital to our world of the early twenty-first century as it was to hers in the twentieth century.

Conclusion

Generations over the past twenty-one centuries have turned to Paul to discover anew how Paul speaks to them in their world. By looking at Paul's spirituality and his spiritual vision, we have endeavored to do the same. While there is so much in the writings of Paul that we could concentrate upon, the four aspects that we have considered are not only central to Paul's spirituality but are also vital for our own spiritual lives as followers of Christ in the twenty-first century.

The cross and resurrection; the transforming power of grace and the gift of the Holy Spirit; the gift of faith and the response of good works; the community of believers as the Body of Christ—these are the hallmarks of Paul's spiritual vision. As I have endeavored to show, they are as well essential dimensions to enliven our own spirituality. However, we have to make them our own. In line with Paul's teaching on the gifts of the Holy Spirit, we realize that each person is unique and has been endowed by the Spirit with different gifts and abilities. It is important to recognize this uniqueness in our own spiritual lives. We are not intended to become carbon copies of Paul. What we do strive to do is to embrace those aspects of his spirituality that are important for us in our journey of faith, and to see how they can transform our spiritual lives, our relationships with Christ, and our relationships with one another in the Body of Christ.

Perhaps a better way to express this thought is to say that Paul's spirituality should teach us to imagine the world with new eyes, to think differently, to think spiritually about our own lives and the world in which we live. As Paul says, "For those who live according to the flesh are concerned with the things of the flesh, but those who live according to the Spirit with the things of the Spirit" (Rom 8:5).[1] Contrast what Paul says here with our own daily lives: What influences us unconsciously each day? What has the greatest impact upon us and our thinking in an unconscious way? This is exactly what Paul refers to as being concerned "with the things of the flesh"—with the material world, with our success, our health, our appearance, our position in society, our jobs, our studies, our work, and a host of many other things. In themselves these things are not bad. The problem is that if that is our focus and aim in life, then we need to have a reality check. Paul's spirituality offers us this reality check.

We can say this another way: *We are what we think.* If we think about material things ("the flesh"), then we are living life solely on the material plane, which is the path to death. If we think about spiritual realities, then we discover the fullness of life, peace, harmony, hope, and joy. As Paul says in the same context, "The concern of the flesh is death, but the concern of the Spirit is life and peace" (Rom 8:6).[2] Paul's spirituality challenges us to expand our horizons, to see that there is more to the world and to life than simply "the things of the flesh." Through the power of the Spirit we are able to see beyond the horizon of a material world, to the spiritual world. We need to look on our material world with eyes of the Spirit. The four hallmarks of Paul's spirituality help us lead life in an enriching and transformative way.

What is your spiritual vision? What energizes your life? What do you feel passionate about? These are vital questions to ask yourself. Let Paul's spirituality give new meaning to your own life and your own spirituality. So that we can look on the world through Paul's spiritual vision and say with the same assurance of Paul:

> In all these things we conquer overwhelmingly through him who loved us. For I am convinced that neither death, nor life, nor angels, nor principalities, nor present things, nor future things, nor powers, nor height, nor depth, nor any other creature will be able to separate us from the love of God in Christ Jesus our Lord. (Rom 8:37-39)

Notes

Introduction—pages 1–8

1. Although thirteen letters are attributed to Paul, most scholars make a distinction between those seven letters that are considered to be authentic as coming from Paul himself (1 Thessalonians, 1 Corinthians, 2 Corinthians, Philemon, Philippians, Galatians, and Romans) and the other six (2 Thessalonians, Colossians, Ephesians, 1 Timothy, 2 Timothy, and Titus) that are seen to come from followers of Paul. Among the many reasons for this distinction is that the thought contained in the latter six letters betrays a later time period. For example, in the authentic letters of Paul, the issues with which Paul grapples are those related to the relationship between the Torah (Law) and Christ, whereas in the other letters the issue largely deals with the relationship between the thoughts of the Gentiles and Christ. For this reason, as well as for the sake of the length of this study, I am limiting my discussion of Paul's spirituality to his authentic letters.

2. *Random House Webster's College Dictionary* (New York: Random House, 1995), 1291.

3. Sandra Schneiders, "Theology and Spirituality: Strangers, Rivals, or Partners?" *Horizons* 13/2 (1986): 266.

4. Gustavo Gutiérrez, *We Drink from Our Own Wells: The Spiritual Journey of a People*, trans. Matthew J. O'Connell (Maryknoll, NY: Orbis, 2003), 52–53.

5. Patrick J. Hartin, *Exploring the Spirituality of the Gospels* (Collegeville, MN: Liturgical Press, 2011), 4–5.

6. Gutiérrez, *We Drink from Our Own Wells*, 53.

7. Hartin, *Exploring the Spirituality of the Gospels*, 6.

8. Gutiérrez, *We Drink from Our Own Wells*, 52–53.

9. Hartin, *Exploring the Spirituality of the Gospels*, 8.

Chapter 1—pages 11–24

1. "Saul" is his Hebrew name, while "Paul" is his Latin name (derived by assonance from the Hebrew name, Saul). The opening of the narrative situates him in Jerusalem and so he is referred to as "Saul." After becoming a Christian and because of his activity in the Gentile world, he is consistently referred to as "Paul"

2. In the next section, "Paul's Call as an Apostle," we will reflect more deeply on the spiritual meaning of this encounter with the risen Lord.

3. Note what Vatican II says on the interpretation of Sacred Scripture in the Dogmatic Constitution on Divine Revelation (*Dei Verbum*): "Since, therefore, all that the inspired authors, or sacred writer, affirm should be regarded as affirmed by the Holy Spirit, we must acknowledge that the books of Scripture, firmly, faithfully and without error, teach that truth which God, *for the sake of our salvation*, wished to see confided to the sacred Scriptures" (11, italics added). This text stresses that "the truth" we take from the account is the religious message that is essential "for the sake of our salvation." Everything serves to express this essential religious message. The meaning of "for the sake of salvation" is what we strive to discover and understand, not the peripheral details or way in which it is being expressed.

4. Pope Benedict XVI, *Saint Paul* (San Francisco: Ignatius, 2009), 22.

5. Gutierrez, *We Drink from Our Own Wells*, 52.

6. Father Robert J. Spitzer was the president of Gonzaga University, Spokane, Washington, from 1998–2009.

Chapter 2—pages 27–40

1. Benedict XVI, *Saint Paul*, 62.

2. "*skándalon*," Frank William Danker, *A Greek English Lexicon of the New Testament and other Early Christian Literature*, 3rd Edition (BDAG), based on Walter Bauer's *Griechisch-deutsches Wörterbuch zu den Schriften des Neuen Testaments und der frühchristlichen Literatur*, sixth edition, ed. Kurt Aland and Barbara Aland, with Viktor Reichmann, and on previous English editions by W. F. Arndt, F. W. Gingrich, and F. W. Danker (Chicago: University of Chicago Press, 2000), 926.

3. Graham Tomlin, "*The Power of the Cross: Theology and the Death of Christ in Paul, Luther, and Pascal*" (Carlisle, U.K.: Paternoster, 1999), 313. I have introduced the italics for the sake of emphasis.

4. See Michael J. Gorman, *Cruciformity: Paul's Narrative Spirituality of the Cross* (Grand Rapids, MI: William B. Eerdmans, 2001), 275.

5. Vincent M. Smiles, "Colossians," *New Collegeville Bible Commentary: New Testament*, ed. Daniel Durken (Collegeville, MN: Liturgical Press, 2009), 641.

6. Benedict XVI, *Saint Paul*, 67.

Chapter 3—pages 41–51

1. Notice this is the source for the greeting that has been recently included at the beginning of the Catholic Mass as an option for the greeting said by the Priest.

2. Gary S. Shogren, "Grace," in *The Anchor Bible Dictionary*, vol. 2, D-G, David Noel Freedman (ed.), (New York: Doubleday, 1992), 1087.

3. David A. DeSilva, "Grace," in *Eerdmans Dictionary of the Bible*, David Noel Freedman, Allen C. Myers, and Astrid B. Beck (eds), (Grand Rapids, MI: William B. Eerdmans, 2000) 524–26.

4. Seneca, *de Beneficiis* 1.4.2.

5. Bruce Malina, "Patronage," in *Handbook of Biblical Social Values*, John J. Pilch and Bruce J. Malina (Peabody, MA: Hendrickson, 2000), 151–55.

6. See chapter four for a development of the relationship between works and faith in the spirituality of Saint Paul.

7. Wilhelm Schneemelcher, ed., *New Testament Apocrypha*, trans. R. McL. Wilson (Louisville: Westminster John Knox Press, 1992), 2:239.

8. See, for example, "But if you do not dispossess the inhabitants of the land before you, those whom you allow to remain will become barbs in your eyes and thorns in your sides, and they will harass you in the land where you live" (Num 33:55).

9. Benedict XVI, *Saint Paul*, 70–71.

Chapter 4—pages 52–66

1. Compare how the word for "righteousness" in Greek is translated into English: *dikaiosynē*: righteousness or justification; *dikaiōs*: being righteous or just; *dikaioō*: I justify or I declare to be righteous; *dikē*: justice.

2. We will discuss the sin of Adam and its consequences in the following chapter five.

3. Paul is using "terminology taken from . . . consistent with the Roman use of prisons principally for holding of prisoners until disposition of their cases" ("*phroureō*," in Frank William Danker, *A Greek-English Lexicon of the New Testament and other Early Christian Literature*, 3rd ed. [Chicago: University of Chicago Press, 2000], 1066–70).

4. See Patrick J. Hartin, *James*, Sacra Pagina 14 (Collegeville, MN: Liturgical Press, 2003), 73–74.

5. Benedict XVI, *Saint Paul*, 82.

6. Pope St. John Paul II, *Centesimus Annus* (encyclical on the Hundredth Anniversary of *Rerum Novarum*, May 1, 1991).

7. This term "cruciform love" is taken from the work of Michael J. Gorman, *Cruciformity: Paul's Narrative Spirituality of the Cross* (Grand Rapids, MI: William B. Eerdmans, 2001), 267. In his work Gorman systematically presents the whole of Paul's spirituality through the lens of the cross.

While this is an insightful and well-presented study, I hesitate to limit Paul's spirituality simply to the shadow of the cross. After all, the cross is meaningless without the resurrection. For Paul, it was the experience of the resurrection that helped him to make sense of the cross. So while there is much to be commended by speaking about "a cruciform love," it is too restrictive and needs to be reconnected with a stress on the resurrection that brings the cross to fulfillment and meaning.

8. *Joint Declaration on the Doctrine of Justification by the Lutheran World Federation and the Catholic Church* (October 31, 1999, paragraph 15). Online at: http://www.vatican.va/roman_curia/pontifical_councils/chrstuni /documents/rc_pc_chrstuni_doc_31101999_cath-luth-joint-declaration _en.html.

Chapter 5—pages 67–73

1. See G. K. Chesterton, *Orthodoxy* (London: Bodley Head, 1957), 9–12.

2. Elliott C. Maloney, *Saint Paul: Master of the Spiritual Life "in Christ"* (Collegeville, MN: Liturgical Press, 2014), 179.

Chapter 6—pages 74–92

1. Note that in Romans 8:5 the New American Bible translates the word *spirit* with a lower case, whereas I have set it as with the upper case *Spirit*. I do this in order to indicate that as a result of the death and the resurrection of Christ, the Spirit of God has now transformed our human spirit empowering it to be able to overcome the weakness of the flesh. The "spirit" is now no longer simply the human spirit, but the power of God's Spirit working through the transformed human spirit that enables it to live in the manner in which Christ has called the believer to live. As Elliott C. Maloney says, "Rather, *pneuma* [spirit] in Paul always refers to a level of being that is transcendent to those who live merely 'in the flesh.' We conclude that Paul *always* considers the activity of the Spirit of God upon the human spirit as an interaction in which both the divine and human partners participate at the deepest level." See Maloney, *Saint Paul*, 82.

2. Benedict XVI, *Saint Paul*, 97.

3. These phrases appear some two hundred times in Paul's undisputed letters (see Maloney, *Saint Paul*, 116).

4. Maloney, *Saint Paul*, 118.

5. The word *Eucharist* is another term not used by Paul. It too developed in the early Church to express the teaching and insights of the Scriptures about the celebration of what Paul calls "the Lord's supper" (1 Cor 11:20) that Jesus instructed his followers to celebrate in memory of his death and resurrection.

6. Benedict XVI, *Saint Paul*, 101.

7. Benedict XVI, *Saint Paul*, 108–9.

8. Andrew Greeley, *The Catholic Imagination* (Berkeley, CA: University of California Press, 2000), 84.

Chapter 7—pages 93–102

1. The name Paul uses frequently, "Christ Jesus" or "Jesus Christ," captures this insight that "the Messiah is Jesus" or that "Jesus is the Messiah." The term Christ (in Greek, *Christos*, and in Hebrew, *Mashiaḥ*, "Anointed One") comes from the Israelite practice of anointing kings at their coronation. The hoped-for Messiah or Christ was to be a descendant of David. Through the Christian liturgy the term Jesus Christ has become the regular designation for Jesus, but in doing so it has lost the original significance and force of the title Christ/Messiah/Anointed One.

2. Benedict XVI, *Saint Paul*, 73.

3. J. Christiaan Beker expresses well the significance of the resurrection for the renewal of creation, "Paul's apocalyptic dualism is not a gnostic dualism of contempt for this world, or otherworldliness. It is determined by the event of Christ, an event that not only negated the old order but also initiated the hope for the transformation of the creation that has gone astray and is in travail because it longs for its redemption from decay (Rom 8:20). Although the glory of God will break into our fallen world, it will not annihilate the world but only break off its present structure of death, because it aims to transform the cosmos rather than to confirm its ontological nothingness." See *Paul the Apostle: The Triumph of God in Life and Thought* (Philadelphia: Fortress, 1980), 149.

4. Virginia Wiles, *Making Sense of Paul: A Basic Introduction to Pauline Theology* (Peabody, MA: Hendrickson, 2000), 134.

Chapter 8—pages 105–33

1. As stated above (chapter 6, note 1), the New American Bible Revised Edition translates the word spirit in a lower case whereas I have set it here in the upper case (Spirit) as it is found in the NRSV translation. The word can be translated either way, but as we have argued throughout, Paul is speaking about the fact that we have become a new creation in Christ and we view the world now through the eyes of God's Spirit.

2. See Pope Benedict XVI's General Audience on Wednesday, January 27, 2010, on Saint Francis of Assisi. Online at: http://www.vatican.va /holy_father/benedict_xvi/audiences/2010/documents/hf_ben-xvi _aud_20100127_en.html.

3. Nancy J. Duff, "Atonement and the Christian Life: Reformed Doctrine from a Feminist Perspective," *Interpretation* 53 (1999), 27.

4. Pope Benedict XVI, homily on the occasion of the canonization of St. Kateri Tekakwitha together with five other new saints on Sunday, October 21, 2012, at the Vatican Basilica. Online at: http://www.vatican.va/holy _father/benedict_xvi/homilies/2012/documents/hf_ben-xvi_hom _20121021_canonizzazioni_en.html.

5. William C. Placher, "Christ Takes Our Place: Rethinking the Atonement," *Interpretation* 53 (1999), 16.

6. Luke Timothy Johnson, *Living Jesus: Learning the Heart of the Gospel* (New York: HarperSanFrancisco, 1999), 201.

7. See, for example, Donna W Brett and Edward T. Brett, *Murdered in Central America: The Stories of Eleven U.S. Missionaries* (Orbis, 1988).

8. John Rosengren, "Father Stan Rother: American Martyr in Guatemala," *St. Anthony Messenger* (July 2006). Online at: http://www.americancatholic .org/messenger/jul2006/feature1.asp.

9. John R. Quinn, Archbishop, "The Relation of Moral Life and Moral laws," *Origins* (May 30, 1996): 29.

10. A good description of the struggles Father Rother faced is found on the website of the Archdiocese of Oklahoma City, "Within the last year of his life, Father Rother saw the radio station smashed and the director killed. His catechists and parishioners disappeared and were found dead after having been beaten and tortured. Father Rother knew all this when he returned to Guatemala in May 1981. It didn't matter. He stayed with his people supporting them in all their needs. He stayed until he was murdered." Online at: http://archokc.org/cause-for-beatification-of -father-stanley-rother/fathers-growing-up-years.

11. *Joint Declaration on the Doctrine of Justification by the Lutheran World Federation and the Catholic Church* (October 31, 1999, paragraph 25). Online at: http://www.vatican.va/roman_curia/pontifical_councils/chrstuni /documents/rc_pc_chrstuni_doc_31101999_cath-luth-joint-declaration_en .html.

12. Richard Marosi, "Sister Antonia Brenner dies at 86; nun moved into Tijuana prison to tend to inmates," *Los Angeles Times,* October 17, 2013. Online at: http://www.latimes.com/local/obituaries/la-me-sister-antonia -brenner-20131018-story.html.

13. Mary Jordan and Kevin Sullivan, *The Prison Angel: Mother Antonia's Life of Service in a Mexican Jail* (Penguin: New York, 2005), 24.

14. Mother Antonia chose her name, Antonia, after a spiritual mentor of hers (Monsignor Anthony Brouwers), who had deeply inspired her and helped her see where God was calling her. He died from spinal cancer in 1964.

15. Jordan and Sullivan, *Prison Angel*, 81.

16. Jordan and Sullivan, *Prison Angel,* 5–6.

17. Jordan and Sullivan, *Prison Angel*, 63.

18. William Yardley, "Antonia Brenner, 'Prison Angel' Who Took Inmates Under Her Wing, Is Dead at 86," *The New York Times*, October 21, 2013, italics added. Online at: http://www.nytimes.com/2013/10/21/us/antonia-brenner-prison-angel-who-took-inmates-under-her-wings-dies-at-86.html.

19. Sr. Consuela Duffy, SBS, *Katharine Drexel: A Biography* (Philadelphia: Reilly Co., 1966), 100. (Official Biography of Katharine Drexel).

20. Peter Finney, The Legacy of St. Katharine Drexel, St. Anthony Messenger, October 2000. Online at: http://www.americancatholic.org/messenger/oct2000/feature1.asp.

21. Cheryl C. D. Hughes, *Katharine Drexel: The Riches-to-Rags Story of an American Catholic Saint* (Grand Rapids, MI: Eerdmans, 2014), 130.

22. Hughes, *Katharine Drexel*, 167.

Conclusion—pages 134–35

1. See chapter 8, note 1.

2. The New Revised Standard Version (NRSV) translates this verse in a much clearer way: "To set the mind on the flesh is death, but to set the mind on the Spirit is life and peace."